दृग् दृश्य विवेक

DṚG DṚŚYA VIVEKA

The Yoga of Seer and seen

An ancient text by Adi Shankaracharya

Commentary by
Clarissa

Dṛg Dṛśya Viveka

www.chup-sadhana.com

yoga@chup-sadhana.com

First published 2009
Revised edition 2010

designed by
www.sndesign.co.uk

ISBN 978-1-4452-0858-9

Printed in the United States of America
via Lulu Press (www.lulu.com)

To Mansoor – thank you

CONTENTS

SHANKARACHARYA

Adi Shankara is known as the *Shankaracharya. Acharya*, has several meanings: a teacher, one who sets the example, one who walks the path.

Adi Shankaracharya, is said to have been born in the southern Indian state of Kerala around 820 AD.The exact date of birth is not known and is often a subject of heated debate in India.

He is the legendary genius, whose name is synonymous with the revival of *Advaita Vedanta* philosophy in India. He was a child prodigy and is said to have mastered the *Vedas* by the age of eight. At sixteen, he is said to have written his commentary on the *Brahma Sutras*. Later he wrote lucid commentaries on the ten principal *Upanishads* and the *Bhagavad Gita*.

His other works fall in the category of *Prakarana Granthas*. These *Prakarana* works are shorter and meant for people who do not have the mental capacity and resources to study his voluminous commentaries on the major scriptures.

This book, *Drg Drsya Viveka,* is one such *Prankarana Grantha*. Some other *Prakarana* books are *Pancadasi, Vivekacudamani, Tattva Bodha.*

Before his death, at the age of thirty-two, *Shankaracharya* founded monastic orders in the four corners of India. These monastic orders have survived and flourished till today, and have inspired many, both in India and outside.

In the last fifty years, there has been a great revival in the teachings of *Advaita Vedanta*. Much of this interest can be attributed to the life and teachings of *Ramana Maharishi* (1879-1950), a great, enlightened Master of the present age. *Ramana Maharishi* was able to re-vitalize the teachings of *Shankaracharya* through his own experience, and turn them into living Truth.

ADVAITA VEDANTA

Advaita means non-dual, and in today's language could be called 'holistic wisdom'.

Vedanta literally means, the end of the *Vedas*. The end of the *Vedas*, can mean, the purpose for which one studies the *Vedas*, and can also mean the *Upanishads*, which form the last section, and are the wisdom aspect of the *Vedas*.

In that sense *Advaita* and *Vedanta* have similar meanings, and are also used together for the philosophy of absolute non-duality.

Advdaita Vedanta can be explained very simply in the following way: most religions agree that before anything was created, before anything happened, there was only the One. After everything comes to an end, when all creation reverts back into its Source, there will also only be that One.

If in the beginning there was only One, and in the end there is also only One, how can there be two in the middle. How can there be a cause other than the One.

In the strife-torn and fragmented world, the vision of *Advaita Vedanta* becomes a wonderful bridge between opposing ideologies. By refusing to see duality in the underlying cause, one can truly live a life of wholeness, one can truly live a life of non-violence.

INTRODUCTION

Drg Drsya Viveka is an ancient Indian scripture attributed to the great sage *Shankaracharya*. '*Drg*' means 'Seer', '*Drsya*' means 'the seen', and '*Viveka*' means discrimination and understanding.

This text deals with the existential question of the relationship between the Seer and the seen, the Knower and the known, the Formless and the form, Being and becoming. The relationship between Awareness and the objects of awareness. It offers no new ideologies, no yogic practices as such, in fact no practices at all. It just shines a light on the most primary aspect that underlies all other aspects of our lives.

The habit of regarding the world and experiences as external to oneself is deeply ingrained. *Drg Drsya Viveka* creates a shift, by turning the attention to 'That', which is knowing the experience. Here, the relationship between the Observer and the observed is transformed. The actions may be ordinary, but that within which they are appearing, is truly extraordinary. This recognition is the *Yoga* of the Seer and the seen.

There is a built-in problem in writing on this subject. When one is writing about Consciousness, one tends to use the word 'it', as if 'it' is a thing to be understood. The one talking about 'it' becomes the subject, and Consciousness is then treated as an object. This is 'setting the cart before the horse'. In fact Consciousness is the Subject and is not a 'thing'. Self is Consciousness.

The question is: how to describe the Indescribable. How to understand That, which cannot be understood. In this commentary Awareness, Consciousness, the Witness, the Seer, the Self, the Formless, the Enlivening Principle, Infinity, Totality, Truth, Context, One Reality, etc are all used interchangeably to point to the Indescribable.

In the *Yoga Sutras of Patanjali*, *Yoga* is described as '*Citta vritti nirodah*', a state in which there are no movements in Consciousness. Consciousness becomes still and clear. In that state, the *Drashtu*, the Seer, becomes aware of Itself. Consciousness becomes aware of Itself as the pristine empty space.

This gap between two thoughts is the state of *Yoga*, and in this gap one becomes aware of oneself as that Consciousness, in which experiences are appearing.

Yoga practices are essentially practices of purification that help to remove the content that has accumulated as baggage from the past. As the content reduces, spontaneously gaps between the thoughts begin to emerge. Understanding happens in these gaps. Consciousness, as the Context, recognizes Itself.

Drg Drsya Viveka is called a '*Prakarana Grantha*'. '*Prakarana*' means chapter or category and '*Grantha*' means a knot, a junction point, a scripture. It deals with one specific category, one specific topic. It is not a well-known scripture. Very few people, even in India, are aware of its existence, as the subject matter is extremely abstract. The subject matter can bring up a lot of resistance. This resistance is the content. This content overshadows the Context.

Here 'content' means all that stuff, which defines the personal identity. 'Context' means that underlying Impersonal Space, within which all the content is appearing. This underlying Space is Consciousness. This is who one really is. This recognition is the whole journey.

The few translations and commentaries that exist on this work are often written from a scholarly perspective. The purpose behind this commentary and translation, however, is to address the thousands of people who are practicing *Yoga* and who have developed some clarity, and in whom the content has been thinned out a little. This will enable them to explore these verses experientially.

Sanskrit scholars may find some discrepancies as the translations are intended more to give the feeling of the meaning. There is also a word for word translation for those who wish to know the meaning of the individual *Sanskrit* words.

Scriptures in the olden days were usually studied in an ashram setting, and amongst people in whom some preparation had already happened. In today's modern world, the places where *Yoga* is practised have become temporary *Ashram* settings.

In *Sanskrit* the word for scripture is '*Sruti*', which means, that which is heard. So the chanting of the scripture is a very important aspect. The vibrations are absorbed deep in the psyche. At the end of this book there is a section with just the verses for chanting.

Over the last 25 years, like many others of my generation, I have tried different techniques and followed many paths. Today I feel that all those paths were important, and have created the preparation necessary to comprehend this scripture. There is a feeling that all paths take one to the same place, and that the different paths may be needed at various stages of one's practice.

There is a feeling of gratitude to all the present and past teachers, who have given me so much. I am especially grateful to Mansoor, the teacher which whom I have studied for the last ten years, who has inspired my love for scripture and has encouraged me to write this commentary.

I am not a *Sanskrit* scholar, but studying *Drg Drysa Viveka* has added a new dimension to my own *Yoga* practice. Scripture opens up a vast horizon of possibility. It is like moving beyond the pull of gravity. For me, writing this commentary has been an incredible journey and a most powerful *Sadhana*.

रूपं दृश्यं लोचनं दृक् तद् दृश्यं दृक्तु मानसम्।
दृश्या धीवृत्तयस्साक्षी दृगेव न तु दृश्यते॥

rūpaṃ dṛśyaṃ locanaṃ dṛk tad dṛśyaṃ dṛk tu mānasam
dṛśyā dhīvṛttayas-sākṣī dṛgeva na tu dṛśyate

The objects of the world are the 'seen' and the eye is the 'Seer'.
In relation to the mind, that eye becomes an object
and the mind its 'Seer'. The Witnessing Consciousness
is the 'Seer' of the movements of the mind.
Consciousness is the real Seer and is not seen by anything else.

rūpaṃ – object, form • *dṛśyaṃ* – the seen, the known
locanam – the eye • *dṛk* – the Seer • *tat* – that
dṛśyaṃ – the seen • *dṛk* – the Seer • *tu* – indeed, but
mānasam – the mind • *dṛśyā* – the seen
dhivrttayahah – movements of the mind
sākṣī – the Witness, Consciousness, Awareness • *dṛg* – the Seer
eva – verily, certainly • *na tu* – but not • *dṛśyate* – the seen

VERSE 1

This verse begins with a simple statement, the eye is the Seer of the objects, and the objects are the seen.

When that same relationship is viewed in terms of the mind and the eye, the mind becomes the Seer of the eye, and the eye becomes the seen.

The different states of mind, the different emotions and attitudes, the different memories and concerns, are constantly appearing and disappearing.

These different states of mind, according to this verse, are known or seen by the *Sakshi*, the Witnessing Consciousness.

Here, the *Sakshi* has become the Seer, the Knower and the conditions of the mind are the seen. This Seer is the real Seer. This *Sakshi* is the Knower of all physical and mental experiences.

The purpose of all yogic practices is to know this Knower.

The problem is that the Knower is the subject, and is not an object of perception. 'It' cannot be an object of the senses or the mind. The Knower cannot be known as a thing or a concept.

To know the Knower, is like asking somebody to stand on their own shoulders.

Knowing the Knower means a state where only knowing remains as the subject, the object and the process of knowing. Only Awareness remains as the observer, the observed and the observing.

The next four verses clarify the fundamental relationship of the Seer and the seen, the Perceiver and the perceived, within which, all the experiences of life take place.

These 31 verses of *Drg Drsya Viveka* take us on a rocket journey from the most ordinary daily experiences, all the way to an understanding of the state of Liberation.

नील-पीत-स्थूल-सूक्ष्म-ह्रस्वदीर्घादि भेदतः ।
नानाविधानि रूपाणि पश्येल्लोचनमेकधा ॥

nīla-pīta-sthūla-sūkṣma-hṛa sva-dīrghādi bhedataḥ
nānāvidhāni rūpāṇi paśyel-locanam-ekadhā

Forms have colours like blue and yellow.
They have qualities like gross and subtle,
and measurements like short and long.
Even though the forms are innumerable,
the eye, as the Seer of all these forms, is One.

nīla – blue • *pīta* – yellow • *sthūla* – gross, rough
sūkṣma – subtle, fine • *hṛa sva* – short • *dīrgha* – long
ādi – etc • *bhedataḥ* – differentiated, differences
nānā vidhāni – many kinds • *rūpāṇi* – forms
paśyet – sees • *locanam* – the eye
ekadhā – remaining the same, unchanging

VERSE 2

In the course of our lives we have seen hundreds of thousands of things with our eyes. We have seen beautiful, wonderful, inspiring things and we have seen horrible, ugly, despicable things.

When one looks at one's eye that has seen all these things, one finds that the eye itself has not changed. The eye, which has seen the vast range of objects, people and events, has not been affected at all.

The knowing of physical reality takes place in all the sense organs; here the eye is just being used as an example, as it is the major highway of perception.

The tongue, which has tasted the wonderful candle-lit dinners, badly cooked food etc, has itself, not undergone any transformation. The ear that has heard sublime music, wonderful compliments and filthy language, itself remains untouched by what has been heard. And so it is with the other sense organs.

The problem in everyday life is that when an object is perceived, all the attention tends to go into that object. The objects and the experiences seem to have a hypnotic effect on us.

We get impressed by both good and bad experiences, and the attention gets hijacked.

The second message that there is also an eye, a sense organ, seeing the object, does not register. The eye, which is the most important factor in the seeing of any object, gets neglected. One finds oneself lost in a world of constantly changing forms and looses perspective of one's Core. The attention being continuously sucked out by all the external events, results in a feeling of deep inner exhaustion.

When we start to also bring the attention to the eye, a feeling of balance happens effortlessly. There is a feeling of bringing the attention back to its Source. Now the attention becomes present in both the object and the subject. There is a harmony between the external and the internal.

This is the first practical step in the understanding of *Drg Drsya Viveka*, the *Yoga* of the Seer and the seen.

When one is hearing words of praise or blame, just by moving the attention to where the sound is touching the ear, an interesting shift in perception takes place. A certain inner imbalance is set right.

Becoming aware of the tongue, while one is speaking has a profound effect on our speech and on the torrent of mental activity. We then tend to not talk so fast, and other people perceive our words as extremely clear and lucid. Communication becomes more refined.

When one is eating, one just becomes aware that there is also a tongue that is tasting the food. When one is hearing a sound, one becomes aware that there is also an ear that is hearing. When one is smelling something, becoming aware that there is also a nose. When one is feeling the environment, becoming aware that there is also the skin, which is feeling the touch of the air.

When one is feeling the breath, becoming aware that one is alive.

आन्ध्यमान्द्य–पटुत्वेषु नेत्रधर्मेषु चैकधा ।
संकल्पयेन्मनः श्रोत्रत्वगादौ योज्यतामिदम् ॥

āndhya-māndya-paṭutveṣu netradharmeṣu caikadhā
saṃkalpayen-manaḥ srotra-tvagādau yojyatām idam

The different conditions of the eye like blindness, weakness or sharpness of vision, are cognized by the one mind. The same happens with the other sense organs like the ears and the skin.

āndhya – blindness • *māndya* – diminished vision
paṭutveṣu – sharp vision • *netradharmeṣu* – conditions of the eye
ekadhā – remaining the same
saṃkalpayet – imagines, projects, cognizes • *manaḥ* – by the mind
śrotra – ear • *tvak* – skin • *ādau* – etc
yojyatām – relates to • *idam* – this

VERSE 3

In the previous verse, the Seer/seen relationship is described in terms of the eye as the 'Seer', and the various forms as the 'seen'. In this verse, *Shankaracharya* goes a step further. The eye in reality is only a lens and an aperture in the head. This physical lens is not the actual Seer. It is the mind that is the Seer, seeing through the eye.

As people become old, they find that their eyesight becomes weak. There are people who are gifted with sharp eyesight, with sparkling eyes, with melancholy or laughing eyes. In all these examples the eye is the object that is being described, and the mind is the Knower.

The same mind as the Knower, knows the other instruments of perception like the ears, the tongue, the nose and the skin. One may say 'my tongue is burning', 'my ear is aching', 'my nose is blocked', or 'the skin is itching'. Here the sense organs and their conditions have become the seen, in relation to the mind.

During deep sleep, when the mind is not active, all the sense organs become inactive. The aches and pains in different parts of the body are not experienced in the state of deep sleep.

Shankaracharya does not use the word 'Seer' for the mind, rather he uses the expression '*sankalpayen manah*', which means the mind that imagines and conceptualizes. The mind is the eye of the eye. What has been viewed by the physical eye gets conceptualized by the mind and then seeing happens.

For example, one arrives home and realizes that one's keys are gone. Automatically, with the mind's eye one starts to retrace one's movements during the day. There may then be a sudden insight. One may see with the inner eye, where one left the keys.

Another example is when talking to a stranger on the telephone and mechanically creating a mental image of that person. When one actually meets that person for the first time, there is often a shock as one realizes that they are completely different from how one had imagined them to be.

During the night when one is dreaming, the physical sense doors are not active. It is the mind that is both creating the images and seeing the images. It is the mind, which is perceiving all that one sees, hears, tastes, smells and feels.

कामः संकल्प–संदेहौ श्रद्धाऽश्रद्धे धृतीतरे।
ह्रीर्धीर्भीरित्येवमादीन् भासयत्येकदधा चितिः ॥

kāmaḥ saṃkalpa-saṃdehau śraddhā-'śraddhe dhṛtītare
hrīr-dhīr-bhīr-ityevam-ādīn bhāsayaty ekadhā citiḥ

The different states of mind: longing, intention, doubt, conviction,
lack of conviction, determination, lack of determination, humility,
understanding, fear etc are all seen in and by,
the light of Consciousness, which itself remains unchanged.

kāmaḥ – longing, desire • *saṃkalpa* – idea, intention
saṃdehau – doubt
śraddhā aśraddhe – conviction / lack of conviction
dhṛtītare – determination and its opposite • *hrīr* – humility
dhīr – understanding, wisdom • *bhīr* – fear
iti evam ādīn – like these, etc • *bhāsayat* – illumines, reveals
ekadhā – remaining as one, changeless • *citiḥ* – Consciousness

VERSE 4

In this verse, *Shankaracharya*, moves further still. Now the mind itself becomes an object of perception.

Various states of mind like happy, sad, bored, fearful, loving, hating etc are continuously arising and passing away. No state of mind is eternal. The mind is never still, it is constantly changing.

Between these ever changing states, however, there are small gaps. These are the gaps between the thoughts. When the thoughts slow down a little, it is possible to become aware of the gaps. In these 'thoughtless moments' one realizes that one is not one's thoughts, one is the 'Knower' of one's thoughts. One is Consciousness.

When thoughts are absent you are not absent, you are still there. The feeling of 'being there' is Consciousness. This 'realization of Consciousness' is being pointed to in this verse.

Consciousness is the screen on which the different thoughts are playing. The thoughts may be 'many' but that which is 'knowing' all the thoughts is not 'many'.

Here Consciousness is the 'Seer' and the mind has become the 'seen'. Consciousness is the ultimate 'Seer' of all that is appearing. People who have understood this verse can try the practice of 'thought-watching'. This is a practice in which one just becomes aware that a thought has arisen, and lets the thought go. Just allowing the thoughts to arise and dissolve, without liking or disliking them. Without interfering with the thought, and without developing a relationship to it.

This practice is possible for a very small percentage of people, because most peoples' minds are a deluge of thoughts. To practice 'thought-watching', one needs some space between the thoughts. This space is stationary and is needed to see the movement of thoughts. This being stationary is the Space of Consciousness.

It is like sitting in an outdoor café and watching the people passing by. To watch the people moving past you need to be stationary yourself.

Different practices like *Yoga*, mediation and chanting help to create space through purification. Purification means the content of the mind, both the good stuff and the bad stuff, gets reduced, gets eliminated. Reducing the content of the mind naturally reveals the Consciousness behind the mind.

नोदेति नास्तमेत्येषा न वृद्धिं याति न क्षयम्।
स्वयं विभात्यथान्यानि भासयेत् साधनं विना॥

nodeti nāstmetyeṣā na vṛddhiṃ yāti na kṣayam
svayaṃ vibhātyathānyāni bhāsayet sādhanaṃ vinā

This Consciousness does not rise, nor does it set,
it does not increase nor does it decay.
All experiences happen in the light of Consciousness.
It appears by itself without any cause and reveals
the world without any effort.

na udeti – does not arise • *na astam eti* – does not set
na vṛddhiṃ yāti – does not increase • *na kṣayam* – does not decay
svayaṃ vibhāti – is self illuminating, self revealing • *atha* – and now
ānyāni – others • *bhāsayet* – reveals • *sādhanaṃ*– any means
vinā – without

VERSE 5

Now Consciousness as the Seer is being described. The Indescribable is being described.

Consciousness is not an object of the senses or the mind. 'It' cannot be described as an object, like a house, or a car or an aeroplane. 'It' can also not be described as an idea, as a feeling or as an emotion. 'It' cannot even be described as wisdom.

Consciousness can only be pointed to. Therefore the only honest statement one can make about Consciousness is '*Neti-neti*', which means 'not this, not this'.

In this verse, *Shankarayacharya* says that Consciousness does not rise, nor does it set. It does not get bigger and it does not get reduced. The danger in talking about Consciousness is, that one inadvertently turns 'It', into an object. When the Subject has been turned into an object, everything becomes upside-down. This is the problem in the study of scriptures.

When it is understood, that Consciousness cannot be 'understood', then real understanding has happened.

Consciousness can only be 'experienced' and cannot be 'known'. Only Consciousness can experience Consciousness. One can only 'be' Consciousness. It is not possible for the mind to grasp something that is beyond the mind.

Consciousness is the experience of one's Self, one's very Existence.

Any attempt to define Self, even the clearest definition, will create a distortion. Self is pure Subjectivity. When the attention has been withdrawn from all externalization, physical or mental, Subjectivity remains as that underlying experience.

Upon waking up in the morning, one does not need another person to tell us that we exist. This feeling of 'I am' appears spontaneously. One is present without any effort. This spontaneous experience of Self-awareness is so natural that one never pays attention to it. Nor does anyone ever remind us about 'Its' existence.

Every morning upon waking up from sleep, we find our world appearing by itself. This extraordinary act of becoming aware, and the world appearing in that Awareness, without any effort on our part, is the great miracle.

One sees this miracle reflected in little babies' expressions when they wake up in the morning, this look of wonder at their own existence and at the world around them. In animals one also finds this exuberance and joy of waking up to the world.

No effort and no techniques are needed to experience oneself as this Consciousness. Consciousness is self-effulgent, it is its own light. In the light of this Consciousness, our world of joys and sorrows appears. All this happens without any effort, without any trying, without any doing.

By simply stopping for brief moments, becoming quiet and resting, we can experience ourselves as Consciousness, as this Underlying Principle.

We can experience this very directly in the gap between the thoughts, the gap between the in-breath and the out-breath, the gap between the actions and events, the gap between sleeping and waking.

चिच्छायाऽऽवेशतो बुद्धौ भानं धीस्तु द्विधा स्थिता।
एकाहंकृतिरन्या स्यात् अन्तःकरणरूपिणी॥

cicchāyā'veśato buddhau bhānaṃ dhīstu dvidhā sthitā
ekāhaṁ-kṛtiranyā syāt antaḥkaraṇa-rūpiṇī

The reflection of Consciousness enlivens the Buddhi.
This enlivened mind then appears in two forms:
as 'I am the doer' and the inner instrument.
As the thinker and the thought.

cit-chāyā – reflection of Consciousness
āveśataḥ – engulfing, enlivening
buddhau – in the natural, pure mind • *bhānaṃ* – appearance
dhīh tu – as the mind • *dvidhā sthitā* – present in two forms
eka āhaṁkṛtih – one as 'I am the doer' • *anyā* – the other
syāt – is • *antaḥkaraṇa* – inner instrument, individual mind
rūpiṇī – in the form of

VERSE 6

There are two philosophical directions from which one can look at this verse. From the perspective of *Dvaita* (dualistic) philosophy, Consciousness and Nature are considered to be two different polarities: *Purusha* and *Prakriti*. *Prakriti* is lifeless, until enlivened by *Purusha*. From this dualistic perspective, this verse is saying that *Purusha* or Consciousness becomes associated with *Prakriti* or the mind principle. The result of this association appears as the *Ahamkara* (personal identity, individual ego self) and the *Antahkarana* (individual mind). In other words the thinker and the thought are born simultaneously.

From the perspective of *Advaita* (non-dual) philosophy, there is only one Self, one Consciousness appearing as both the individual and the world. The thinker and the thought are only two aspects of the same Consciousness.

Whether one approaches from the dualistic or the non-dualistic philosophy, the purpose of all practices is the same. The practices are a reverse journey to the Source from which the *Ahamkara* emerges. This is the Source from which the thinker and the thought appear, from where a personal, individual consciousness is born and from where the Formless takes on a form.

Ahamkara has no corresponding word in the English language and is usually translated incorrectly as 'ego'. Actually 'ego' has a completely different meaning.

'*Aham*' literally means 'I', as undivided Consciousness, and '*Akara*' means a shape or a form. So *Ahamkara* means the formless, shapeless unlimited Consciousness, appearing as a shape with limitations. To believe I am a man or a woman is *Ahamkara*. To believe I am young or old, fat or thin, beautiful or ugly is *Ahamkara*. To believe I am a doctor or an engineer, Indian or English, is *Ahamkara*.

Ahamkara means 'I am a form' and 'I am the doer'. The battle going on in everybody's head is the *Ahamkara*, as the thinker, trying to control the *Antahkarana*, as the thoughts.

As one develops in the inner practice, moments of pure Awareness appear. In these moments there is an experience that this 'me', who I think I am, and my thoughts, originate from the same place. That place is Consciousness, before it splits into the thinker and the thoughts. When it is seen that my likes and dislikes, and who I think I am, are one and the same, the bundle that is *Ahamkara* starts to unravel.

One way to understand *Ahamkara* is by looking at what we experience when we dream at night. The dreaming consciousness associates with the content of the mind. This association gives rise to various kinds of dreams. The many personalities that appear, and also who we think we are in the dream, are produced by this contact of Consciousness with the content of the mind. These may be impressions left from the day before, or may be deep impressions left from past lives.

In Indian philosophy there is a fascinating technique called '*Vad*' and '*Apvad*', which is sometimes used to point to the Indescribable. '*Vad*' means a doctrine, a point of view, a philosophical direction. '*Apvad*' means the opposite, a negation of the doctrine, the non-existence of that point of view.

In this scripture something similar is being done. The next seven verses explain *Ahamkara*, and describe it as a separate reality, as something tangible, as somebody real. Then from the twentieth verse onwards the whole idea of *Ahamkara* is completely negated. It is shown that no such thing as an *Ahamkara* exists. This is '*Apvad*', negation.

For people who think logically it may appear absurd, to first build a premise and then demolish it. Why build it in the first place?

If we go a little deeper, we see the point. For example, one can talk of infinite space because there is the understanding of the limited space of a room. One can describe a room and the space in the room in great detail: the size, the height, the back or the front of the room. However, once there is a clear conviction of the reality of the space of the room, the walls and the ceiling lose their relevance. One realizes suddenly that there is no room and there never was a room. It was always all one undifferentiated space. Only because of limitations called walls and ceiling, had the concept of a room taken shape.

The space outside the room and the space inside the room, were never separated. No special glue is needed to join the two spaces. The removal of the limiting concept of walls automatically reveals infinite space.

Another example is that of a glass. Everybody is aware of the space in a glass. The space may be around 200ml and it may be a tall or a wide glass. What very few people see is that the glass also exists in space. The space in the glass and the infinite space, in which the glass exists, are exactly the same. They have the same nature. By only giving value to the space in the glass, one ignores the vast space, as the context.

Similarly, *Ahamkara* as a body/mind structure is the limitation that creates the illusion of a separate consciousness. The positive side of the limitation is that the limited can reveal the Unlimited. Then the limited has served its purpose.

Otherwise how should Infinity know Itself. When Infinity is all that there is, when there is nothing other then That, how should That know Itself.

The important point is that in Indian philosophy, *Ahamkara*, as an ego self is not considered bad or evil. It is only the Infinite Consciousness taking on a form. Forms are needed to play the games of life. The drama of life needs good actors and they must identify with their roles.

In that sense, all of us are perfect actors because our original nature as God is so well hidden behind the masks that we are all wearing. Hardly ever do we see the mask, the *persona* slip, and perceive the Divine in the other.

छायाऽहंकारयोरैक्यं तप्तायः पिण्डवन्मतम् ।
तदहंकारतादात्म्यात् देहश्चेतनतामगात् ॥

chāyā'haṁkārayor-aikyaṃ taptāyaḥ piṇḍavan-matam
tadahaṁkāra-tādātmyāt dehaś-cetanatām-agāt

The aliveness of Consciousness, appearing as the Ahamkara,
due to identification, then enlivens the physical body.
In the same way as a heated iron ball appears to glow.

chāyā – reflection (of Consciousness)
ahaṁkārayoh – ego, conditioned self
aikyaṃ – becoming identified • *taptāyaḥ* – hot iron
piṇḍavat – like a ball • *matam* – is considered
tat ahaṁkāra – that ego • *tādātmyāt* – due to identification
dehaḥ – the body • *cetanatām* – Aliveness, Consciousness
agāt – has gained

VERSE 7

The example that is used in this verse is of an iron ball that has been placed in a hot fire for a period of time. This iron ball, when removed from the fire, appears to be bright and glowing.

Brightness, heat and formlessness are the qualities of fire. Blackness, coldness and heaviness, are the qualities of iron. The combination of the two produces a third entity, a hot, glowing iron ball, which is neither iron nor fire, or is both iron and fire.

Consciousness is another word for aliveness. Consciousness identified with the individual personality, enlivens it. One could also say that the aliveness of Consciousness is the 'life' in an individual person. An individual personality is like a blueprint. Blueprints are many, but the Enlivening Principle is one and the same.

The example of electricity, illustrates this point. In one's home there are many different electrical appliances performing all sorts of functions. Some heat the house, some make it cool, some provide light etc. However, behind all the different functions, there is only one enlivening principle. The usefulness of all the appliances is dependant upon the same electric current running through them. If the electricity does not enter the appliance, the appliance is useless.

Consciousness, associated with *Ahamkara*, enlivens the physical body, bringing energy, vitality and brightness. When Consciousness exits the body, the body becomes lifeless. Then one sees that the only thing of value in anybody is Consciousness, as life itself.

The problem with the reading of the verse is that *Ahamkara* and Consciousness are said to come together and get identified. That there are 'two' creates a philosophical hazard. Later in this scripture, one sees how there is only Consciousness. Consciousness itself becomes *Ahamkara*.

To say that Consciousness has identified with the mind is like saying that gold has identified with the gold ornaments. In fact, the ornaments are only modifications of gold. The ornaments are nothing but gold. Take away the gold and there are no ornaments.

अहंकारस्य तादात्म्यं चिच्छायादेहसाक्षिभिः ।
सहजं कर्मजं भ्रान्तिजन्यं च त्रिविधं क्रमात् ॥

ahaṁkārasya tādātmyaṃ cicchāyā-deha-sākṣibhiḥ
sahajaṃ karmajaṃ bhrāntijanyaṃ ca trividhaṃ kramāt

Consciousness, identified with Ahamkara,
appears in the body in three different conditions:
natural, attached to action and attached to delusion.

ahaṃkārasya – of the ego • *tādātmyaṃ* – identity
cit chāyā – the reflection of Consciousness
deha sākṣibhiḥ – in the body and the Witness
sahajaṃ – natural, effortless
karmajaṃ – with a motive, born of action
bhrāntijanyaṃ – born of delusion, ignorance
ca – and • *trividhaṃ* – is of three kinds
kramāt – respectively

VERSE 8

This verse explains how this One Consciousness manifests in the world of name and form as three distinct modes of expression.

In Indian philosophy the entire world of phenomena, or *Prakriti* is seen as the interplay of the three *Gunas*, or qualities. These three qualities are known as *Sattva* or clarity, *Rajas* or activity and *Tamas* or ignorance. These three qualities correspond to three modes of expression *Sahajam*, *Karmajam* and *Bhrantijam*.

The body, mind, personality, thoughts, emotions, liking, disliking, the food that we eat, and everything else, is said to be made up of these three *Gunas*. Therefore it is said that the entire universe is nothing but the *Gunas* playing with the *Gunas*. An endless play of light, of scattering and of darkness.

The only 'thing' that is not made up of these three *Gunas*, is 'That' which is aware of the three *Gunas*. Awareness or Consciousness.

Only Awareness is free of this constantly changing kaleidoscope.

Sahajam, means born of effortlessness, and relates to the quality of the *Sattva Guna*. In this state, the quality of Consciousness is not completely over-shadowed. Life is seen as a beautiful play in which one is dancing one's part.

There is a natural, easy, present, uncontrived, quality of clarity. There is a lightness and translucency. One feels this quality around little children and in people who are at ease with themselves.

Karmajam and *Bhrantijam* mean to be born of action and delusion. These two represent the *Gunas* of *Rajas* and *Tamas*. *Rajas* has the quality of activity, motion, desire, excitement, deep liking and disliking etc. *Tamas* has the quality of heaviness, inertia, sleep, laziness, forgetfulness etc.

These two *Gunas* of *Rajas* and *Tamas* appear in our lives as obsessive, compulsive actions, which are based on delusion. These are the two qualities most prevalent in society. Actions feed the delusion, and delusion feeds further actions. It is like a cat going round and round forever chasing its own tail.

The three *Gunas* are present in everything and in everybody. Depending on which *Guna* is in excess, we may call a person *Sattvik*, *Rajasik* or *Tamasik*.

Even food may be *Sattvik*, *Rajasik* or *Tamasik*, depending on the effect it has on us. The same goes for the environment and the vibrations of a certain place. These qualities also apply to *Yoga* teachers, *Yoga* students and different practices.

The *Yoga* practice helps to reduce the qualities of *Rajas* and of *Tamas*. The patterns of continuous action and delusion get thinned out, and the *Sattva Guna* becomes more predominant. When *Sattva* is present, comprehension takes place spontaneously. Even a few lines from a scripture can make a deep impression. A person in whom *Sattva* is predominant will have a certain luminosity, clarity and a powerful Presence.

After a *Yoga* class one may feel very light, very clear, as if clouds have been dispersed. This is a very direct experience of the *Sattvik* state. The events of one's life, which appeared so burdensome just a couple of hours ago, may for a short while, have simply vanished. In reality the events have not changed, the *Gunas* have changed.

This is the main reason for the popularity of *Yoga* practices. *Yoga Asanas* create deep purification in the body and the mind. The group energy in *Satsang* or in a *Yoga* class is also very helpful, as the *Sattvik* aspect increases for everybody. This is also the reason why there may be a deep longing to go to an *Ashram* or on a spiritual retreat, to find some quality of *Sattva*.

Living in modern society, and still maintaining a *Sattvik* state, is almost impossible unless one has some daily practice.

संबन्धिनोस्सतोर्नास्ति निवृत्तिस्सहजस्य तु ।
कर्मक्षयात् प्रबोधात् च निवर्तेते क्रमादुभे ॥

saṃbandhinos-sator-nāsti nivṛttis-sahajasya tu
karma-kṣayāt prabodhāt ca nivartete kramād-ubhe

The uncontrived relationship between the Ahamkara and Consciousness does not come to an end till the end of one life. The other two relationships gradually come to an end with the exhaustion of karma and the dawning of wisdom.

saṃbandhinoḥ – relationship, identification
satoḥ – between the two • *nāsti* – cannot happen
nivṛttiḥ – ending • *sahajasya* – natural, uncontrived
tu – but • *karma* – action, impressions
kṣayāt – exhaustion, depletion
prabodhāt – with knowledge, awakening
ca – and • *nivartete* – come to an end
kramād – respectively, gradually • *ubhe* – the other two

VERSE 9

The word '*Sambandha*' means to relate and also means the product of that relationship. The most primary of all relationships is the relationship between Consciousness and *Ahamkara*. This relationship of the Formless with the form is described in the previous verse as *Sahajam*, *Karmajam* and *Bhrantijam*.

In reality there is no relationship. It is like saying the relationship of gold to the ornaments. If one were to get too excited by the design of the ornaments, the relationship with the gold may be over-looked. One may talk of the ornaments as having a reality of their own. One may compare one ornament with another, and make judgements.

To exist, means to exist in a form. When one stands in front of a mirror, a reflection is produced in a mirror naturally. This is the effortless natural relationship between the body and Consciousness.

This primary relationship between the form and the Formless in its natural state is not a problem. The form exists to express the Formless, and the Formless needs a form to express itself. This uncontrived relationship does not come to an end as long as one is alive. This relationship is called *Sahajam*.

When one watches small children there is a feeling of this naturalness. A feeling of Consciousness simply expressing through the little bodies. This spontaneous relationship to the form continues, even in the case of great, enlightened masters.

Karmajam and *Bhrantijam* manifest as the obsessive actions one performs, based upon delusion of one kind or another. *Karmajam* or born of *Karma* has two different meanings. One meaning is *Karma* from previous lifetimes, which one has to fulfil until that *Karma* gets exhausted. The other meaning of *Karma* is simply action.

Bhrantijam, means born of delusion. The biggest delusion is that happiness lies outside oneself. One works from morning to night desperately trying to find that happiness. Chasing rainbows.

This delusion of seeking outside oneself for wholeness, comes to an end when understanding dawns. The relationship based on actions comes to an end when the actions are exhausted.

When one begins a *Yoga* practice, or any other path of

purification, *Rajasik* and *Tamasik* tendencies in us start to reduce. The constant cycle of craving and aversion slows down, and there are moments of feeling comfortable in one's skin. As if the burden of life has been removed. Many traumatic memories, and anger that had got impregnated into the tissues of the body, get released.

The habit of living in the past, with all the regrets attached to it, and trying to reach an imaginary goal in the future, with all its anxieties, comes to an end.

Sometimes people hear of the benefits of *Yoga*, but get worried that they may get too detached from daily life, and may no longer be able to function in the world. How will they pay their rent? How will they interact with their family? How will they do their work?

This verse is clarifying that only those actions based on delusion and compulsiveness come to an end. Whatever is natural to us and to our situation, will continue unhindered. In fact, if it is our destiny and even if we wanted to, we would not be able to change it.

अहंकारलये सुप्तौ भवेत् देहोऽप्यचेतनः ।
अहंकारविकासार्धः स्वप्नस्सर्वस्तु जागरः ॥

ahaṁkāra laye suptau bhavet deho-'pyacetanaḥ
ahaṁkāra-vikāsārdhaḥ svapnas-sarvastu jāgaraḥ

In deep sleep, Ahamkara gets dissolved
and the body appears lifeless.
In the dreaming state, Ahamkara is only semi-manifest.
In the waking state it is full blown.

ahaṁkāra – ego • *laye* – dissolved, absorbed
suptau – in deep sleep • *bhavet* – becomes • *dehaḥ* – the body
api – also • *acetanaḥ* – lifeless, unconscious • *ahaṁkara* – ego
vikāsārdhaḥ – semi-manifest • *svapnaḥ* – dreaming state
sarvaḥ – completely, fully • *tu* – indeed • *jāgaraḥ* – waking state

VERSE 10

The *Ahamkara* is a bundle of likes and dislikes, and is never quiet. The likes and dislikes give rise to judgements, opinions, projections, regrets, desires and aversions etc. Take away the likes and dislikes, and no *Ahamkara* remains.

In the state of deep sleep, Consciousness is said to move to its home in the heart and becomes separated from the patterns and programs. When Consciousness separates from these patterns, *Ahamkara* disappears. The Formless separates from the form and no *Ahamkara* is left.

This is a clear way of indicating both the existence and the non-existence of *Ahamkara*. We cannot say that *Ahamkara* does not exist because it is encountered everywhere. We also cannot say that *Ahamkara* exists because in deep sleep, it is not there.

In the same way we can say that waves exist, because we can see them on a lake, when there is a storm. The same waves are found to be non-existent, when the storm has subsided and the lake is peaceful again.

In the state of meditation, this process happens consciously. One withdraws one's attention from the habitual patterns of the mind, by bringing it to a single point of focus. Consciousness separates from the multitude of patterns, and is no longer fragmented.

Consciousness then becomes aware of itself. This is the feeling of fullness, that people on the spiritual path experience. This is Self-realization.

The important point made in this verse is that a mild state of Enlightenment, a state in which the *Ahamkara* is absent, is experienced by us every night in deep sleep. The happiness we feel upon having had a deep sleep is coming directly from the same Source.

A person can do without food, and even without water, for long periods of time, and still survive, but a person will not survive for long with extended sleep deprivation. The rest of deep sleep is essential to the healthy functioning of mental and physical balance. This experience of being in a state where the *Ahamkara* is not manifest is essential to one's very existence. Here one's existence means the link with the Source.

In the dream state, *Ahamkara* is only partially manifest. It tends to be fairly innocent. That is why many spiritual traditions work with the dream state, because the *Ahamkara* is easier to break through as the resistance is not so strong. *Ahamkara* in the dream state is not so cunning and devious.

In the waking state, *Ahamkara* is said to be in full bloom. The *Ahamkara*, as the waking personality, is manipulative and extremely complex. The feeling of a separate, personal, conditioned identity becomes like a brick wall. This thick wall makes sure that no idea that threatens its existence can ever get through. Especially spiritual knowledge, which is designed to demolish *Ahamkara*, becomes a great threat.

One may consider oneself to be on a spiritual path, or belong to a religious group, but these are mostly only more sophisticated *Ahamkara* games. That is perhaps why the fattest egos are often found in religious organizations and spiritual ashrams.

The constant tension between opposites that the *Ahamkara* needs to survive, is what most of us experience as the noise in the head. That is why all the talk of peace is just another excuse to start a war. True peace is the state when *Ahamkara* has melted. What is left is the Immaculate state of Self. This is 'the peace that passeth understanding'. The increasing of inner Silence, the reducing of thoughts and fewer battles in the head are the real signs of spiritual progress.

Sometimes the stranglehold of the *Ahamkara*, is experienced as a burning in the heart, where several desires are fighting with each other. The *Ahamkara* must maintain this constant tension otherwise there may be a feeling that one is dying. Like dying of boredom.

The nature of *Ahamkara* is to doubt and question the motives of others. It is rare to find a person, in whom *Ahamkara* has started to question *Ahamkara*. This is a sign of true opening.

When one starts to question 'who is this *me* that is having the doubt', the attention turns from the question to the questioner. This is the path of Self-inquiry.

In the *Yoga* practice, when one is experiencing the body in the present moment, *Ahamkara* dissolves. *Ahamkara* gets fattened by past & future. The present moment is like the needle that bursts the balloon of *Ahamkara*.

When *Ahamkara* dissolves, both oneself and the world are experienced as appearing in the One Consciousness. Nothing is separate from oneself. Nothing exists but Self.

We may enter these different states of Consciousness spontaneously in our *Yoga* practice, in an *Asana* or in the final relaxation of *Shavasana*. In *Shavasana*, the posture of a dead body, we can experience this very directly. We are doing nothing, we are just observing the journey of the breath moving through the body, and the weight of the body on the ground, consciously relaxing each part of the body, and letting go of all tensions.

Here we have the opportunity of experiencing the same benefits as in deep sleep. We may gradually move out of the gross physical body. The senses withdraw from contact with the external objects, and we move to subtler bodies beyond the mere physical and mental dimensions. There may be a weightlessness of the body, or it may seem that the body disappears. Awareness temporarily becomes disengaged from the physical and mental realm of existence.

अन्तःकरणवृत्तिश्च चितिच्छायैक्यमागता।
वासनाः कल्पयेत् स्वप्ने बोधेऽक्षैर्विषयान् बहिः।

antaḥkaraṇa-vṛttiśca citicchāyaikyam-āgatā
vāsanāḥ kalpayet svapne bodhe-'kṣairviṣayān bahiḥ

Consciousness identified with the content of the mind,
projects images inwards in the dreaming state.
In the waking state the content is projected outwards,
with the eyes, as the external world.

antaḥkaraṇa – inner instrument, the mind
vṛttiḥ – movements of the mind
citih chāya – reflection of Consciousness
aikyam – oneness, becoming one • *āgatā* – having attained
vāsanāḥ – impressions, desires • *kalpayet* – imagines, projects
svapne – in the dream state • *bodhe* – in the waking state
akṣaih – with the eyes • *viṣayān* – objects • *bahiḥ* – outside

VERSE 11

The word *Vasana* has two meanings. One meaning is to reside, to reside as a desire. The other meaning is smell or fragrance. The complexes and patterns that reside in the deeper levels of our mind, in the so-called unconscious mind, are called *Vasana*. Another name for *Vasana* is *Samskara*.

When we pass through different experiences in life, the experiences sooner or later come to an end, but a certain impression is left behind. Memory of that experience is one aspect of that impression, however behind the memory, we may feel something more subtle. A subtle craving or a subtle aversion, a certain smell or fragrance is left behind. These subtle desires and aversions live in the depth mind, and become the seeds of future actions. These actions and reactions, in turn create new seeds, and the cycle goes on endlessly.

There are innumerable *Vasanas* that live in the depth of the mind in a dormant state. Depending on the conditions and the environment, a particular *Vasana* may get activated, and come to the surface of the mind. When the *Vasana* comes to the surface, it is called a '*Vritti*'. *Vritti* literally means a movement. The *Vasana* that was dormant, now becomes a movement, and expresses itself as an action or reaction, as craving or aversion.

In this verse *Shankaracharya* says, that during the dream state, Consciousness gets identified with a *Vritti* of the mind. Depending on the quality of the *Vritti*, a dream is produced in Consciousness, plays out in Consciousness, and is seen by Consciousness. Consciousness is the scriptwriter, the director, the producer, all the actors and also the audience.

In the waking state, he says, exactly the same process happens, but with the eyes open. Based upon the content of the mind, different *Vrittis* come up to the conscious level to be experienced. When we feel excited, restless, bored, or upset, different *Vrittis* are playing on the surface of the mind. Basically every thought running through our head is a *Vritti*. When we think of the number of thoughts that we have in just a few minutes, we become aware of our predicament.

Consciousness identifies with the *Vritti* and experiences are produced. Depending upon the quality of the *Vritti*, different realities, pleasant or unpleasant, are experienced. This process is identical to what happens in the dream state.

The difference in the waking state is that the experiences are projected outwards, as if there is a reality that is external to Consciousness. In relation to a dream, it is easy to accept that Consciousness itself has become all the characters in the dream, all the physical and mental experiences, all the good and bad that has happened. In the waking state, there is a deep conviction that there is a reality outside us, and that this external reality is separate from us. Upon waking up from a dream, one realizes that the inside and the outside in a dream, were both actually an inner experience. Similarly in the waking state, inside and outside are both appearing in Consciousness, which is neither inside nor outside.

When we look at a film reel, all the characters in the movie exist within the same celluloid. The good guys, the bad guys, the cars, the locations etc, everything is made up of the same thing. When a movie runs in the cinema and is projected on a screen, for a short while, it becomes a living reality.

When we learn to sit quietly and become aware of ourselves

as Awareness, this understanding becomes clear. Whatever is appearing is appearing in Awareness. Since Awareness, in the unidentified state, is clear, empty and immaculate, whatever is appearing in Awareness, is also clear, empty and immaculate.

In this state one has the feeling, that everything is interconnected, everything is the same, everything is Sacred, everything is God. A dry leaf on the pavement and a work of art, or a skyscraper, all appear as being of the same Essence. Not that the shapes are not different, but that in which they are appearing, is the same.

Using the example of a mirror is one way to understand this. Without a mirror, there are no images. Even when the images are in the mirror, they are not really in the mirror. All the different images in the mirror are made up of the same substance. Even when the reflections appear in the mirror, the mirror does not lose its essential empty nature. It is always empty, and exists beyond the images.

Similarly, Consciousness, whether in the dream state or in the waking state, does not lose its immaculate, pristine nature, when different dreams and events play on it. No matter how messed up one's circumstances may be, 'That' in which the circumstances are appearing, is not messed up.

As far as practice is concerned, simply feeling oneself as Awareness, in which the events of life are happening, is enough. Learning to observe the *Vrittis*, the different moods and tendencies that keep coming to the surface, instead of reacting to them, is the practice. In fact there are only two choices. Either we observe the *Vrittis* without reacting to them, as much as possible, or we get identified with them, and start drowning in the experience.

मनोऽहंकृत्युपादानं लिङ्गमेकं जड़ात्मकम्।
अवस्थात्रयमन्वेति जायते म्रियते तथा॥

mano-'haṃkṛtyupādānaṃ liṅgamekaṃ jadātmakam
avasthātrayam-anveti jāyate mriyate tathā

The phantom self, born of the play of the mind,
which in reality does not exist,
goes through the waking, dreaming and sleep states,
and is born and dies.

manaḥ – mind • *ahaṁkriti* – ego
upādānaṃ – constituted, made up of
liṅgam – phantom self, pain body • *ekaṃ* – one
jadātmakam – lifeless and non-existent
avasthātrayam – three states, waking dreaming and sleeping
anveti – pass through • *jāyate* – is born
mriyate – dies • *tathā* – and

VERSE 12

This verse addresses the questions: who is it that experiences the three states of Consciousness: waking, dreaming and sleeping? And who is it that enters and leaves the body, is born and dies?

Consciousness becomes the *Ahamkara* and the mind, the thinker and the thoughts. The thinker and the thoughts, through constant inter-action, produce a feeling of a personal self. This personal self engages in various activities, becomes the dialogue in the head, and over time starts to feel very solid, very real.

A good way to understand what is being pointed to, is again by taking the example of a dream. During a dream, who one thinks one is, is not who one really is in the waking state. A specific imaginary self is produced, based upon the requirements of that particular dream. An imaginary self, conditioned by the dream. This imaginary self, goes to sleep in the dream, drinks coffee, meets friends, travels the world, escapes from danger and may even die in the dream. Upon waking up, this imaginary self is found to have never really existed.

The word '*Linga*' means distinction, or specific signs of

uniqueness, and is applied to this feeling of 'me'. The 'me' in everybody is convinced that somehow it is different from everybody else. There is a feeling of uniqueness about one's circumstances and the events of one's life. This feeling of 'me' appears like a substantiality in the body. When 'I' am insulted, or 'I' am praised, there is a feeling that 'somebody' has been insulted or praised.

This 'me', this personal identity, is a phantom self and is the illusion. It is that which moves through the three states of Consciousness, waking, dreaming and sleeping. This feeling of 'me' as the subtle body, by association, gets transferred to the physical body.

The purpose of different practices is the unravelling of this 'me', which *Shankaracharya* says is not real in the first place. Experiencing oneself as Awareness, as the unmodified Consciousness, before it splits into the thinker and the thoughts, is the effortless practice. As one experiences oneself as the One Consciousness, in which both the feeling of 'me' and 'my concerns' are arising, the friction between these two gets reduced. The phantom self, which is the product of that friction, then gets weaker and eventually dissolves.

शक्तिद्वयं हि मायाया विक्षेपावृति रूपकम्।
विक्षेपशक्तिर्लिङ्गादि ब्रह्माण्डान्तं जगत् सृजेत्॥

śakti-dvayaṃ hi māyāyā vikṣepāvṛti rūpakam
vikṣepaśaktir-liṅgādi brahmāṇḍ-antaṃ jagat sṛjet

The mysterious power of becoming, called Maya,
expresses in two ways:
as the power of projection and the power of veiling.
Creation produces everything, all the way from the individual self
to the entire Universe.

śakti – powers, impulses • *dvayaṃ* – two • *hi* – indeed
māyāyā – of Maya • *vikṣepāvṛti* – creation and veiling
rūpakam – expressions • *vikṣepaśaktir* – creating power
liṅgādi – personal separate self etc • *brahmāṇḍa* – entire universe
antaṃ – the end of • *jagat* – the world • *sṛjet* – creates

VERSE 13

A new word '*Maya*' is introduced in this verse. People familiar with Indian philosophy understand *Maya* as illusion, as the play of Consciousness. The word *Maya* is composed of two syllables '*Ma*' and '*Ya*'. '*Ma*' means 'not' and '*Ya*' means 'is'. Therefore one of the meanings of *Maya* is 'that which is not'.

Behind the play of *Maya* there is only One Consciousness, which is responsible for the whole show. The purpose of these verses is to lead one back to that Source, where the illusion is dissolved.

In this verse *Maya*, the creative aspect of Consciousness, is said to have two powers: the power to create multiplicity, and the power to obscure the Source. Saying that *Maya* has two powers, is like saying that fire has two powers, to illuminate and to heat.

In *Vedanta* philosophy an example used to point to the relationship between *Maya* and Consciousness, is the sun and the clouds.

The sun creates the clouds by causing the water of the ocean to evaporate. These same clouds that are formed, then conceal the sun.

In other words, *Maya* is not an enemy of Consciousness, is not something evil, not something bad. It is just Consciousness at play. Water is called ice when it freezes but is essentially just water.It has just been given a different name due to its new quality and expression. So it is with *Maya,* which is simply the expression of Consciousness in action.

The creative power of *Maya* is responsible for the appearance of the personal 'me' mentioned in the previous verse. This same creative power is responsible for the entire universe, for the entire world of becoming. All the way from a blade of grass to the highest celestial realms.

This verse is pointing to the paradox that the 'personal me' and 'my world' are both a creation of that which is not.

The veiling aspect of *Maya* is the ability to conceal the single Source, just as the clouds conceal the sun. This veiling of the single Source creates a feeling of separateness in everybody and is what allows all the dramas of life to take place. If this veiling power were not there, there would not be any relationships, any friends nor any enemies. Everywhere Self would see Self, and the play of life could not go on.

In the same way, as a magician on the stage has the ability to produce all kinds of objects out of thin air, and also the ability to keep the audience from seeing how the tricks are done, the force of *Maya* makes the tricks of life appear real, by obscuring their Source.

From a practice point of view, *Maya* is a synonym for *Ahamkara*, the separate self. All relationships begin with an individual 'I', who then gives rise to a 'you'. This gives rise to a 'he, she, they, them etc'. When the hardness of the *Ahamkara* melts, through whichever practice, one starts to experience oneself as not separate from one's environment, and not separate from one's world. This melting creates a beautiful harmonious effect. Others start to appear softer and one will feel a deep compassion for all beings. In whatever way one sees oneself, one will also see others.

People sometimes say that 'everything is Maya', that everything is an illusion, and therefore 'what is the point in doing anything.' More correctly, the separation and duality that one sees, is *Maya*. Behind the illusion of multiplicity, is the reality of the Source.

सृष्टिर्नाम ब्रह्मरूपे सच्चिदानन्दवस्तुनि ।
अब्धौ फेनादिवत् सर्वनामरूपप्रसारणा ॥

sṛṣṭir nāma brahmarūpe saccidānanda-vastuni
abdhau phenādivat sarva-nāma-rūpa-prasāraṇā

The entire universe, appearing as names and forms, is Brahman.
The ingredients are Sat, Chit and Ananda.
In this Unconditioned Reality, the world of names and forms
is just like a little foam on the edge of the ocean.

sṛṣṭih – creation • *nāma* – is the same as
brahmarūpe – the nature of Brahman, Infinite
saccidānanda – Existence – Consciousness – Bliss
vastu – ingredient, substance • *abdhau* – in the ocean
phenādivat – like foam • *sarva* – all
nāma-rūpa – name and form • *prasāraṇā* – the flowing, manifesting

VERSE 14

In this verse the cat is finally out of the bag. All the preceding verses have been a preparation to hear this verse.

The entire universe, everything there is, is *Brahman*.

The word *Brahman* comes from the root '*Brh*', which means big. *Brahman* is not the name of a personal God of a religion, it simply means the Universal, the Final Reality, the Highest Truth. In the *Upanishads*, *Brahman* is said to be that, which can only be described in negatives, as '*Neti-neti*', which means 'not this, not this'. To make any positive statement about *Brahman* would be to limit the Unlimited.

In this verse *Shankaracharya* says that *Srishti* or creation, is *Brahman*. Whatever exists, at whatever level, in whichever reality, is *Brahman*. The entire play of the universe is *Brahman*. In the physical reality, whatever we see, hear, touch, taste, smell is *Brahman*. In the mental reality all the thoughts, emotions, feelings, hopes, desires, fears etc are all *Brahman*.

The next phrase is '*Satchidananda vastuni*'. The universe is made of *Satchitananda*. *Satchitananda* is a combination of three words: *Sat*, *Chit* and *Ananda*, and is used as a synonym for Brahman.

'*Sat*' means absolute Truth, beyond truth and untruth. '*Chit*' means Awareness, Consciousness, the Knowing Principle. '*Ananda*' means that happiness, which is beyond happiness and unhappiness.

What is being said here is quite incredible. The entire creation, with all its contradictions, with all its imperfections, with all its wars and its exploitation, disease and death, is made up of *Satchitananda* or Absolute Truth, Consciousness and Unconditioned Bliss.

In this verse a new concept '*Nama Rupa*' is introduced. *Nama Rupa* means name and form, body and mind. To exist means to exist in a form. *Nama Rupa* is the world of multiplicity. *Nama Rupa* means the individual lives, the billions of life forms.

In Indian philosophy even a rock is *Nama Rupa*. *Nama Rupa* as present in every aspect of creation. Thoughts, feelings, emotions and ideas are all included in *Nama Rupa*.

All creation, from the grossest to the subtlest, is *Nama Rupa.*

Nama Rupa is a synonym for *Maya. Nama Rupa* represents the diversity in creation. Everything appears to be separated from everything else.

In the next line, the entire field of name and form is compared to foam on the edge of the ocean. The ocean is the Unconditioned Vastness of Being, and the world of names and forms are just like a little foam on the edge of this Vastness.

The purpose of this verse is to move the attention from the pettiness of the foam, to the Vastness of the Ocean.

From the perspective of practice, Consciousness is the Vast Ocean, and the events that are happening in life are like the foam that comes and goes. Moving the attention away from the 'content' as the experiences of life, to the 'context' as Awareness, is all that is needed.

The world of duality is created by liking and disliking. The slightest preference splits the wholeness in Awareness. It is not that we do not see a dog and a cat as different, rather it is a way of looking, in which one is also seeing the one space, within which both are appearing. Or one could say that both are appearing in Awareness, which is essentially empty and pure.

When it is understood that the Highest Reality, *Brahman,* and the individual consciousness are one and the same, then there is not much left to understand.

अन्तर्दृग्दृश्ययोर्भेदं बहिश्च ब्रह्म सर्गयोः ।
आवृणोत्यपरा शक्तिः सा संसारस्य कारणम् ॥

antar-dṛkdṛśyayor-bhedaṃ bahiśca brahma sargayoḥ
āvṛṇotyaparā śaktiḥ sā saṃsārasya kāraṇam

The other force of Maya, the veiling Shakti,
is responsible for obscuring the distinction between
the Seer and the seen within, and Brahman and creation outside.
This is the cause of Saṁsara.

antaḥ – within, in oneself
dṛkdṛśyayor – between the Seer and the seen
bhedaṃ – the distinction, the separation
bahiḥ – outside • *ca* – and
brahma – Brahman, the Infinite, the Unchanging
sargayoḥ – creation, world of becoming • *āvṛṇoti* – obscuring, veiling
aparā – the other • *śaktiḥ* – power, force • *sā* – it
saṃsārasya – of Samsara • *kāraṇam* – is the cause, reason

VERSE 15

The previous verse gave a glimpse of that radiant, transcendent Reality that underlies everything. In this verse the veiling power of *Maya* is exposed. The veiling power which conceals the radiance of the Truth.

Even though the world that we live in is appearing in Consciousness, and is not other than Consciousness, it gets projected outside and we feel it is separate from us. This is the first aspect of veiling.

Externally the world of name and form is seen as a constantly moving phenomena, and That which is unmoving is not seen. This is the second aspect of veiling.

Everybody is constantly in motion, trying to reach somewhere, trying to fulfil desires and to find peace. This constant becoming and changing, creates new relationships, new destinies and new lives. This vast kaleidoscope of shifting realities, both individual and collective, is called *Samsara*.

In one of the *Upanishads*, *Samsara* is described as '*Samsarati iti Samsara*', which means 'that which is constantly shifting'. The entire *Samsara*, as the world of multiplicity, is the result of this veiling. When the veil is removed *Samasara* comes to an end.

From a practice point of view, that which is knowing the changes, is itself not a change. The Awareness of a sound, is not a sound; the Awareness of a colour, is not a colour; the Awareness of a taste, is not a taste. Awareness which is knowing all the different conditions, is itself not a condition.

Shifting back to Awareness is the practice.

When one learns to look as 'nobody', one also starts to have a sense of 'That', in which events are appearing. Only a 'nobody' is able to experience the Nameless and the Formless. When one looks as 'somebody', everything is seen as fragmented and separate.

In the way we perceive the world we create *Samsara*. One can say that not being present creates *Samsara* because *Samsara* exists in time. That which is Timeless is not *Samsara*.

In some scriptures, *Maya* is treated as the energy of *Brahman*, the creative power inherent in Consciousness. In these scriptures, *Maya* is worshipped as the Divine Mother. *Radha-Krishna*, *Sita-Ram*, *Shiva-Shakti*, are the metaphors to point to this mysterious relationship between Being and becoming.

As the creative aspect, *Maya* creates the universe out of her own Being, and it is she herself, who becomes the universe. She becomes the elements of the universe and enters all the different forms. She becomes the sun, the moon, the stars and the fire to illuminate the universe that she is creating. It is She who becomes the *Prana*, the vital force, to keep all creatures alive. She becomes the food and water, to satisfy our hunger and quench our thirst. Whatever we see or don't see, whatever exists, from a blade of grass to the highest celestial plains, is the creation of *Maya*. It is that supreme energy, which moves and animates everything. Even though She enters each and every creature that She creates, She never looses Her identity or Immaculate Nature. From this perspective, one does not try to come out of *Maya,* rather one surrenders with the understanding that *Brahman* and *Maya* are the same.

साक्षिणः पुरतो भति लिङ्गं देहेन संयुतम्।
चितिच्छाया समावेशात् जीवः स्याद् व्यावहारिकः॥

sākṣiṇah purato bhāti liṅgaṃ dehena saṃyutam
citicchāyā samāveśāt jīvaḥ syād vyāvahārikaḥ

Consciousness in close proximity to the Witness
enlivens the subtle body and the gross body.
This identification of Consciousness with the form
gives rise to an embodied transactional being.

sākṣiṇaḥ – the Witness • *purataḥ* – close to, filled with
bhāti – shines, enlivens • *liṅgaṃ* – the subtle body, phantom self
dehena – the gross body • *saṃyutam* – identified
citicchāyā – the reflection of Consciousness
samāveśāt – due to entering • *jīvaḥ* – the embodied self
syād – and becomes • *vyāvahārikaḥ* – the transactional being

VERSE 16

In this verse *Shankaracharya* points to the birth of the transactional self. This transactional self is the person we all experience and consider ourselves to be in day-to-day life.

Two new words come up here, '*Jiva*' and '*Vyvaharikah*'. '*Jiva*' means a living being, an individual. '*Vyvahara*' in *Sanskrit* means behaviour or the way one acts, therefore '*Vyvaharikah*' means the one who is acting out the various roles.

This is the one who is inhibited, gets embarrassed and does not think he/she is good enough. This is the one who craves attention, who shows off, who talks too loudly in restaurants and on their mobile phone.

When one answers the phone, depending on who is calling, one has to take on a certain identity. The one taking on all the different identities of sister, friend, wife, daughter, mother, employer, employee etc is the empirical or transactional self. '*Vyvaharikah*' refers to the one who is behaving in different ways, in different situations, and is playing the different roles. During the day as we slip from one role into another, there is a feeling of a 'me' who is moving through these different roles.

The same Consciousness enlivens both the mind and the body. Consciousness is the same but the thought patterns, with which it is identified, are constantly changing. That is why even in the same person, different transactional selves are continuously being born to deal with different situations, as the need arises. We are all superb actors and very skilled at playing multiple roles.

The other aspect of Consciousness is the subtle *Prana* that is responsible for the activity of the physical body. *Prana* and Consciousness are two sides of the same coin. By moving one, the other moves automatically. *Prana* is easier to feel in the physical body. The way people walk, talk, work and move about, are all indications of the quality of *Prana* and the level of Consciousness.

In the practice of *Hatha Yoga*, one uses *Asanas* to shift the *Prana* from the lower *Chakras* into the higher *Chakras*. Activating the higher *Chakras* allows more refined and subtler states of Consciousness to be experienced.

Watching the natural flow of the breath is a complete practice in itself. The breath is always 'here and now' and is an actual physical experience. It acts as a bridge between the physical body and the mind.

This observing of the natural breath develops present moment Awareness, sharpens the instrument of attention, and purifies the mind. The mental curtain of obsessive patterns and distortions gets reduced, and 'That' which has been hidden, is revealed. The breath is like an invisible thread that leads one directly back to the Source.

अस्य जीवत्वमारोपात् साक्षिण्यप्यवभासते।
आवृतौ तु विनष्टायां भेदे भातेऽपयाति तत्॥

asya jīvatvam-āropāt sākṣiṇyapyavabhāsate
āvṛtau tu vinaṣṭāyāṃ bhede bhāte-'payāti tat

The transactional self, due to superimposition,
obscures the Infinite Consciousness.
When the veiling comes to an end, the illusion disappears
and Consciousness shines naturally.

asya – this • *jīvatvam* – the individuality
āropāt – superimposed • *sākṣiṇi* – in the Witness • *api* – also
avabhāsate – appears • *āvṛtau* – veiling • *tu* – but
vinaṣṭāyāṃ – is destroyed • *bhede* – the difference
bhāte – shines, becomes clear • *apayāti* – goes away • *tat* – that

VERSE 17

This verse talks about the mystery of becoming. How the veiling power, inherent in Consciousness, turns the Impersonal into a personal identity. How this conditioned self, born of Consciousness, manifests as an individual. How this individual goes through the ups and downs of life, and through the vast complexity of experiences.

This separate personality, born of imagination, gets superimposed on Consciousness, which is the real Self. In Indian philosophy this is the original sin, and the original pain. All other pains derive their existence from this primal pain. Without the ending of this delusion, suffering cannot come to an end. In other scriptures this is called '*Mula Avidya*' or root ignorance, which is blocking and veiling the Truth.

Whatever good or bad, that has happened in one's life, that one has done in one's life, is based upon this single delusion. When the veil is removed, the underlying Impersonal Consciousness is seen as the single cause of everything.

An example used in *Vedanta* is that of the snake and the rope. In the evening twilight a farmer is walking back from his field and happens to step on a rope. In the half-light, the rope is mistaken for a snake. The poor farmer runs away in fear, imagining himself to have been bitten by the snake. However, upon investigation, no snake is found, only the rope is discovered.

In Indian philosophy, the individual personality is also seen as a superimposition. It is described as neither false, nor real. One cannot say it is false, because it is experienced in every day relationships. One can also not say it is real, because upon investigation it is not found. Also every night, during deep sleep, it is absent.

The important thing is that behind the illusory snake, there is a real rope, and even when the snake is being seen, there is still only rope. All practices are started by this illusory self, and all practices are designed to dissolve the one who starts the practice.

When Consciousness becomes one-pointed, it acts like a laser-beam that cuts through that dusky, flickering darkness. This is the darkness of living in the past and the future, the endless mad dialogues running in the head, the neurotic fears and desires, projections, hopes, regrets, idiosyncrasies etc.

The scriptures of *Hatha Yoga* use the term '*Kundalini*' instead of *Maya*. *Kundalini* is both the veiling power of Consciousness, and also the revealing power. The *Kundalini Shakti* in its dormant state veils and deludes, and the same *Shakti*, when awakened, brings Liberation and Illumination.

When this *Kundalini Shakti* is awakened by the practice of *Yoga*, it cuts through the delusion of the duality of *Maya* and reveals the One Reality. The conscious and the unconscious minds dissolve back into the Source.

Consciousness merges into Consciousness.

The *Yoga Sutras of Patanjali* say '*Samadhi-siddhir Ishvara pranidhanat*' (ch 2 sutra 45), which means that perfection in *Samadhi* happens when one surrenders to God. Here all disappears. The meditator, the practice and the space in which the practice is taking place, disappear.

Only Divinity remains. This is how the *Bhakti* or the devotional path leads to the same point of Oneness.

तथा सर्गब्रह्मणोश्च भेदमावृत्य तिष्ठति ।
या शक्तिस्तद्वशाद्ब्रह्म विकृतत्वेन भासते ॥

tathā sarga-brahmaṇośca bhedam-āvṛtya tiṣṭhati
yā śaktis-tadvaśād-brahma vikṛtatvena bhāsate

In the same way, due to force of the veiling power,
the world of multiplicity over-shadows the one Reality,
and it appears as if the Unchanging is changing.

tathā – in the same way
sarga-brahmaṇoh – of the world of form and Brahman
bhedam – distinction • *āvṛtya* – covering • *tiṣṭhati* – is established
yā – which • *śaktis* – the (veiling) power
tadvaśād – due to its force
brahma – Brahman, the underlying Reality
vikṛtatvena – as though changing • *bhāsate* – appears

VERSE 18

On a full moon night, the moon is reflecting on the water of a lake. The breeze in the air is creating ripples in the water. When looking at this reflection of the moon, it may appear as if the moon is moving. However it is the movement of the water that has been superimposed on the reflection of the moon, making it appear to be dancing.

When sitting in a stationary train at a railway station and another train on the neighbouring platform starts moving, it may appear as if the train in which one is sitting, is the one which is moving.

The ocean appears to be composed of many different waves, but it is just one mass of water, and the waves whether large or small, are just an expression of the water as they arise and disappear.

These examples illustrate the process of superimposition.

The primary superimposition is the world of phenomena imposed on *Brahman*. Behind the joys, the wonders, the suffering, death, starvation and all the neurotic compulsive actions, there is only Awareness, which is empty, pristine and immaculate.

The previous verse and this verse indicate how the activities of the conditioned reality get superimposed on the unconditioned Consciousness. The white screen in the cinema allows many different kinds of movies to be seen. The movies may be funny, boring, tragic or romantic. The screen, however, does not undergo any modification.

The comparison of the screen with Consciousness is only an example, not to be taken too literally. The difference is that the screen is passive, and the images are projected on it from somewhere else. With Consciousness however, Consciousness produces the movies, reflects the movies, acts in the movies, sees the movies, analyses the movies, and then reacts to its own analysis.

Consciousness is the magic screen out of which all things emerge.

अत्राप्यावृतिनाशेन विभाति ब्रह्म-सर्गयोः ।
भेदस्तयोर्विकारः स्यात् सर्गे न ब्रह्मणि क्वचित् ॥

atrāpyāvṛti-nāśena vibhāti brahma-sargayoḥ
bhedastayor-vikāraḥ syāt sarge na brahmaṇi kvacit

The destruction of the veiling reveals the distinction between the world of becoming and Brahman.
It is then seen that changes take place in creation and not in Brahman.

atrā api – here also • *āvṛti* – veiling • *nāśena* – due to destruction
vibhāti – reveals, shows • *brahma* – Brahman, the underlying Reality
sargayoḥ – in creation • *bhedaḥ* – separation, differenece
tayoḥ – of the two • *vikāraḥ* – modification, changes • *syāt* – is
sarge – in the world of becoming
brahmāṇi – in Brahman, in the one Reality • *na kvacit* – not ever in

VERSE 19

In this verse *Shankaracharya* talks of the destruction of the veil. The veiling power that creates the division between the individual, and the Totality. The veiling that is the root of all misery and despair.

The veil is made up of everything that one considers oneself to be. The entire bundle of 'contents', which becomes like an iron curtain around the individual. One gets deeply identified with these contents and can spend a lifetime rationalizing one's story, and defending one's beliefs.

The point is being repeated here, that the purpose of all practices is to destroy the veil that is covering the Truth. Truth is present everywhere, here and now, at all times, in everybody. One does not have to seek Truth, one only has to find out what is creating the separation.

Separation begins with 'me'. Then continues with 'you, he, she, they, them,' and 'my world' is born, in which the 'I' gets lost. By seeking my own Source, by seeking the Source of the 'I' feeling, one discovers the Universal Consciousness that pervades everything. Here no personal 'I' is found. Instead of removing the suffering, one removes the sufferer. Suffering cannot exist without the sufferer. A 'somebody' suffers. 'Nobody' cannot suffer.

This is called Liberation when there is nobody left to be liberated.

In the practice of *Yoga*, one learns to watch the body without concepts, just as it is. These initial steps are very important, because if one cannot even feel one's body without judgement, how will one ever be able to witness one's thoughts.

Watching effortlessness is a peculiar experience. The body is working and obviously there is effort in the posture, but the mind is still. A magic moment comes when one just slips into the Witnessing Consciousness. One leaves behind past and future. The *Asana* just is, and there is only the present moment. This can also be called the experience of *Samadhi*, when one is in a state of doing nothing and wanting nothing, one is just witnessing the body and the mind performing their respective functions.

One starts to experience oneself as the unbroken Stillness, whether one is performing an *Asana*, or resting between the postures. Time exists as a movement of the mind and when one slips out of thoughts, there is the experience of Timelessness. The underlying Consciousness is unbroken and has no beginning and no end.

अस्ति भाति प्रियं रूपं नाम चेत्यंश-पञ्चकम्।
आद्यत्रयं ब्रह्म रूपं जगद् रूपं ततो द्वयम्॥

asti bhāti priyaṃ rūpaṃ nāma cetyaṃśa-pañcakam
ādyatrayaṃ brahma rūpaṃ jagad rūpaṃ tato dvayam

Whatever exists has five aspects:
existence, appearance, dearness, name and form.
The first three aspects point to Brahman,
as the one unchanging Reality,
the latter two, point to the world as multiplicity.

asti – is, isness, existence • *bhāti* – shines, Consciousness
priyaṃ – dearness, lovable • *rūpaṃ* – form, shape
nāma – name • *iti aṃśa pañcakam* – these are the five aspects
ādyatrayaṃ – the first three • *brahma* – Brahman
jagad – world of multiplicity, of duality • *tataḥ* – the latter
dvayam – two

VERSE 20

From a practice point of view, this is the most important of all the verses in this scripture. Here *Shankaracharya* says that whatever exists, individually or collectively, is made up of five aspects.

The five aspects are divided into two groups, *Brahman* and *Jagat*. So actually the five aspects are two aspects. As we go further we find that there are not even two aspects. It is an either or situation. When *Brahman* is seen, *Jagat* is not seen, and when *Jagat* is seen, *Brahman* is not seen.

Brahman means the undifferentiated, unconditioned One Truth. *Jagat* means the universe of names and forms, the world of multiplicity. Therefore when the One is seen, many are not seen, and when many are seen, the One is not seen.

When one experiences *Asti*, *Bhati* and *Priyam*, then the Underlying Truth, *Brahman* is being experienced. When *Nama Rupa* are being experienced, then it is the world of multiplicity.

'*Asti*' means 'Is' or 'Isness. The 'Isness' of any object, of any form is the 'Being' aspect. Whatever 'Isness' is seen in any form, important or unimportant, is Brahman. Even the 'Isness' of a grain of sand on the beach is Brahman.

'*Bhati*' means to shine, to appear. For anything to appear there must be light, and that light, is the light of Consciousness. So whenever we see something, that 'seeing' is pointing to the Consciousness aspect of one's Self.

'*Priyam*' means very dear, the source of Bliss. When something or somebody in the world is dear to us, the love that we feel towards that person is the love inherent as our own Self.

Asti, *Bhati*, *Priyam* is another way of expressing *Satchitananda*. *Sat* is Being, *Chit* is Consciousness and *Ananda* is Bliss. When it is clearly understood that other than Consciousness, there is no external world, then every experience in life can be used to return to the Source.

When looking at any object, instead of seeing the name and form, one can concentrate on the 'Isness' of it. One needs to do this for a few minutes before the experience of 'Isness' inside starts to be felt. Similarly looking at the 'appearance' of any object for several minutes, will also make us feel like something is awakening in us. When either of the first two practices are done, the third experience of Bliss arises spontaneously.

When one looks at the world as an individual, as somebody with a name and form, one will only see other individuals, and other names and forms. Name and form is a synonym for judgement, and the individual personality is only a bundle of judgements.

Moving through life as a name and form, one experiences oneself as separate from the Totality. In this state of separation, the universe is projected outwards, and one sees a vast world separated from oneself. This gives rise to a feeling of deep loneliness, incompleteness and yearning. This yearning is projected out into the world of multiplicity, and the result is endless *Samsara*.

The *Asti*, *Bhati*, *Priyam* aspect, which *Shankaracharya* calls *Brahman*, cannot be experienced by a fragmented individuality. Only Wholeness can experience Wholeness. Only the Unconditioned can experience the Unconditioned. In fact, the personal identity, who one thinks oneself to be, is the only blockage to experiencing this Oneness.

Hatha Yoga uses *Asana, Pranayama* and concentration, to create purification in the body and the mind. This purification untangles and removes congealed patterns, beliefs and memories in us, and allows the Consciousness to become translucent and clear.

People who practice *Yoga* regularly may experience this feeling of openness, and a willingness to absorb new perspectives. There is a feeling of expansion and permissiveness, as opposed to contraction and rejection.

खवाय्वग्निजलोर्वीषु देवतिर्यङ् नरादिषु।
अभिन्नास्सच्चिदानन्दाः भिद्यते रूपनामनी॥

khavāyvagni-jalorvīṣu devatiryaṅ-narādiṣu
abhinnās-saccidānandāḥ bhidyate rupanāmanī

The five elements, space, air, fire, water and earth;
gods, animals and humans etc are all only undifferentiated
Truth-Consciousness-Bliss.
They only appear to differ due to names and forms.

kha – space • *vāyu* – air • *agni* – fire • *jal* – water
urvī – the wide one, earth • *deva* – in gods • *tiryaṅ* – in animals
narādiṣu – in human beings etc • *abhinnāḥ* – are the same
sat-cit-ānandāḥ – Truth – Consciousness – Bliss
bhidyate – appear different • *rupanāmanī* – the name and form

VERSE 21

In Indian philosophy the entire creation, including the mind and thoughts, is said to be made up of the interplay of the five elements called '*Prapanch*'. '*Kha*' is the space element, '*Vayu*' is the air element, '*Agni*' is the fire element, '*Jal*' is the water element and '*Urvi*' represents earth. These five elements are the raw material of the entire physical and mental spectrum.

The five elements, which means everything in creation including *Deva*, *Tiryan* and *Nara*, meaning 'the gods, animals and human beings' are all nothing but *Satchitananda*, Being-Consciousness-Bliss.

The entire realm of existence is encompassed here. There is nothing in creation that is not *Satchitananda*.

The last two words '*Bhidyate Rupanamani*' means 'name and form create separation'. The practice is to see an object or a person without getting impressed by the name and form. To see the 'Isness' and appearance of an object, without labelling it, without naming it, without calling it mine or yours.

In other words, to see an object without the mind, without

the past, and without the conditioning.

One way to practice this is to take any object and look at it continuously for about five minutes. Just looking without creating a strain on the eyes, but looking persistently. In the beginning, the thoughts relating to the object will come up. As one continues looking, without getting distracted, the number of thoughts will gradually reduce. Then a moment may come when there is just looking. There is just the 'Isness' of the object, and the 'Isness' of the one looking.

One can start the practice by looking at ordinary objects: a piece of rock, a glass or a flower. Don't try to push the thoughts away. Just keep looking at the object continuously. After some time the thoughts and the mental process get exhausted, and only the existence and appearance of the object remains.

One can take any object, internal, external or even a thought form. By putting the attention strongly on it for several minutes, one can dissolve the concreteness of that object and experience its impersonal nature.

The Essence will remain, the *Asti*, *Bhati*, *Priyam* will remain.

When one goes around labelling and defining things, one is

actually covering up the Bliss of *Brahman* that is inherent in each experience. The present moment, when experienced without labels from the past and future, becomes full of Aliveness and Bliss. Then one realizes that labelling and naming are extremely costly propositions.

In the *Yoga* practice, one simply experiences the body, the breath etc, as it is. One does not try to describe, define or improve anything. One hears the sounds, feels the sensations without the string of associations, as if for the first time.

The posture becomes unimportant, it is the *Satchitananda* concealed in the posture that is the real reason we practice. Once this doorway is opened the practice takes on a different flavour.

उपेक्ष्य नामरूपे द्वे सच्चिदानन्दतत्परः ।
समाधिं सर्वदा कुर्याद् हृदये वाऽथवा बहिः ॥

upekṣya nāmarūpe dve saccidānanda-tatparaḥ
samādhiṃ sarvadā kuryād hṛdaye vā-'thavā bahiḥ

Ignoring the names and forms,
seeing Satchitananda as the highest,
Samadhi is the experience all the time,
in the heart or outside.

upekṣya – ignoring, not being impressed
nāmarūpe – names and forms • *dve* – both
sat-cit-ānandāḥ – Truth – Consciousness – Bliss
tatparaḥ – devoted to the highest
samādhiṃ – meditation • *sarvadā* – all the time
kuryād – should do • *hṛdaye vā* – either in the heart
āthavā bahiḥ – or outside

VERSE 22

This verse is a continuation of the previous one. Simply being indifferent to the name and form, and giving importance to Awareness, in which the name and form is appearing, is the practice. Indifference to name and form does not mean that we don't see the differences in our day-to-day life. It means to develop the penetrating power of vision to see beyond the name and form.

One may also try to do this looking, with intense attention at another person, but instead of looking at their form, and all that one may associate with that form, one shifts the attention slightly to look at the space around them. One may experience their form to simply disintegrate, and only light remain. This is what happens when one sees a person's Aura.

One learns to look through the superficialities right to the Essence. The point is to look beyond, and to look from a state of Consciousness, which is free of beliefs and baggage. Clarity in oneself can then see Clarity in the other.

Another method is to sit in a room in front of a mirror. The light should be indirect, or slightly dim. One looks continuously at one's image in the mirror, without creating tension in the eyes. As one keeps looking, a point may come when the mirror will be seen as empty. One may experience one's reflection as having disappeared.

In the second line *Shankaracharya* says that when one is experiencing oneself as Consciousness, wherever one goes, whether physically or mentally, one will always be in a state of *Samadhi*. *Samadhi* is the eighth and last limb of *Yoga*.

When we understand that whoever we are seeing, is appearing in Consciousness, then we understand the importance of looking without judgement. Whatever judgement we are making about the other, is creating a split in our own Consciousness. Just as in a dream, if we are hating someone, we are actually only hating ourselves. Whoever we reject in the dream, we are only rejecting ourselves.

Therefore by ignoring the name and form, and seeing wholeness, one is creating the experience of wholeness as one's own Consciousness. This wholeness of Consciousness is *Samadhi*.

Shankaracharya continues to say that this practice can be done both inside and outside. This is an important point, that even the internal objects, like thoughts, emotions, feelings can be seen in the same way as external objects. The ability to see ones own thoughts appearing in Consciousness may take some time to develop, because the habit of fighting with one's own thoughts is deeply ingrained.

Initially one may need to keep bringing the attention back to the heart, as a point of focus. When the mind stops jumping, the attention just remains in the heart. In time one will experience the heart, not as any particular physical location, rather as the seat of Being.

This is not something that can be done, this is the natural state, which happens spontaneously when all the doing, thinking, defining and trying to understand come to an end.

This is an effortless process, *Sahaja Samadhi*, just resting as Awareness in whatever comes up.

सविकल्पो निर्विकल्पः समाधिर्द्विविधो हृदि ।
दृश्य शब्दानुविद्धेन सविकल्पः पुनर्द्विधा ॥

savikalpo nirvikalpaḥ samādhir-dvividho hṛdi
dṛśya śabdānuviddhena savikalpaḥ punar-dvidhā

The two practices of meditation in the heart
are either with an object or without an object.
Objects of meditation are again of two kinds:
using a form or using a sound.

savikalpaḥ – with an object, with a support
nirvikalpaḥ – without an object, without any support
samādhiḥ – practices of meditation • *dvividhaḥ* – of two kinds
hṛdi – in the heart, within • *dṛśya* – the seen • *śabda* – with words
ānuviddhena – supported by • *punaḥ* – is again
dvidhā – two kinds

VERSE 23

Starting with this verse, six different practices are being talked about. They can be called practices of convergence. Consciousness, which was fragmented, due to the many desires and concerns, is now brought back to the state before the fragmentation. One may use different supports to bring about this convergence, depending on one's nature and circumstances.

These six practices that are described, are strictly speaking, not practices, rather insights. Interestingly, *Shankaracharya* uses the word *Samadhi* instead of *Dhyana*. *Dhyana* means meditation and *Samadhi* is the fruit of the meditation.

The six practices can be understood using the analogy of a movie screen. Let us say that a movie screen, on which films are playing non-stop, becomes tired of continually experiencing itself as the movies, and wants to experience its essential nature as a clear, empty, pristine, still screen. The movies by their nature are moving. There are exciting action movies, followed by boring movies, by tragedies, comedies etc. Let us say that the screen has heard that essentially it's own nature is flawless and immaculate.

As far as practices go, the screen really has to do nothing to experience itself to be the same nature as the clear light in the projector. All the efforts and practices are to decrease the intensity of the movies, and perhaps to find some gaps between the movies. Or perhaps simply to stop playing the movies, full of excitement, terror and fear.

In that sense one can say that no practices are needed to experience one's Essential Nature. At the same time one understands that practices are absolutely necessary.

The root meaning of the word *Samadhi* is a state of equanimity. *Samadhi* is a combination of two words '*sam*' and '*dhi*'. '*Sam*' means to equalize, a state where convergence happens. The word '*dhi*' refers to the mind, to Consciousness. Therefore *Samadhi* can be called the practice of bringing about the state of convergence. The state where the scattered mind has come back together, the mind has become One.

Savikalpa and *Nirvikalpa* are technical terms for two kinds of *Samadhi* mentioned here. '*Vikalpa*' means a concept or a notion. Therefore '*Savikalpa*' means with an object, with a support. It is a practice in which there is the duality of the meditator and the object of meditation.

Savikalpa Samadhi, or meditation with a support, is then further divided into two categories. One kind uses the 'seen' as an object of practice, and the other uses 'sound'. Objects used in meditation are usually some mantra, an image, a yantra, or the breath. In fact any object, on which one can focus easily, can be used as a support.

Nirvikalpa Samadhi comes up in verse 26 and refers to advanced practices, where Awareness itself becomes the object of Awareness. The meditator and the meditation merge into each other, and nobody is left to meditate. At this stage all effort comes to an end.

We can understand *Savikalpa Samadhi* and *Nirvikalpa Samadhi* using the analogy of a rocket launched into outer space. For the rocket to lift off and break out of the field of gravity, an enormous amount of power and effort is required. Once the rocket has broken through the gravitational field, its requirement of power becomes zero. In that sense we can say that *Savikalpa*

Samadhi uses some support and a lot of effort to control the wild fluctuations of the mind. When some purification has happened, gaps between thoughts emerge spontaneously, and in these gaps Awareness becomes aware of Awareness. This is *Nirvikalpa Samadhi*.

Whether it is *Savikalpa* or *Nirvikalpa*, the experience of *Samadhi* is the same state of Oneness in the heart.

कामाद्याश्चित्तगा दृश्याः तत्साक्षित्वेन चेतनम् ।
ध्यायेत् दृश्यानुविद्धोऽयं समाधिः सविकल्पकः ॥

kāmādyāś-cittagā dṛśyāḥ tatsākṣitvena cetanam
dhyāyet dṛśyānu-viddho-'yaṃ samādhiḥ savikalpakaḥ

Longings and thoughts arising in the mind are the seen.
Being aware of these movements of the mind,
as their Witness, is meditation supported by form.

kāmādyāḥ – desires, longings etc • *cittagāḥ* – born in the mind
dṛśyāḥ – are the seen • *tatsākṣitvena* – as their Witness
cetanam – Consciousness
dhyāyet – one should meditate, put one's attention on
dṛśyā – the seen • *ānuviddhaḥ* – related to • *ayaṃ* – this is
samādhiḥ savikalpakaḥ – the practice of meditation with form

VERSE 24

The first type of *Savikalpa Samadhi* is described here.

A normal person's mind is like a movie theatre that never shuts down. Thoughts are constantly appearing and there is a continuous struggle between them. Good thoughts are trying to control the bad thoughts.

In this practice, one turns these disturbing, agitated thoughts into objects of meditation. These thoughts, no matter what their content or quality, are treated as movies, and one considers oneself to be the screen upon which they are appearing and disappearing. Actually the screen has no real relationship with the movies, and one just considers oneself to be the uninvolved Witness watching the show.

The purpose of this verse is to indicate that one is actually Consciousness, the screen upon which the thoughts are appearing. Instead of trying to change the thoughts, or remove the thoughts, or to have better thoughts, one shifts into a space of watching.

If one likes a thought, there will be a reaction. If one dislikes a thought, there will be a reaction. If one justifies a thought, there will be a reaction, and reactions always mean more thoughts.

To put it simply, the way out is not to get impressed by one's thoughts. This watching of thoughts, without reacting, reduces the number of thoughts, and automatically gaps start to open up, between the thoughts.

In these gaps one becomes aware of oneself as the 'Context' in which the thoughts as the 'content', are appearing. Simply by treating the turmoil in the mind as the 'seen' and abiding as the 'Seer' becomes the practice.

One can start the practice of thinning out the thoughts, by trying a simple exercise. One just notices 4 or 5 sounds around one. Just observing the different sounds for a few minutes, and then enquiring 'Am I these sounds?' One will see that one is not the sounds, but is the one who is 'knowing' the sounds. This Knowing is Consciousness. The sounds have a beginning and an end, but the Knowing is unbroken.

Similarly one can experience oneself as the 'Knower' of the breath. One can then feel the environment, around one, feel the body, feel the sensations, feel the touch of the air on the skin etc. Just watching as it is, without liking or disliking, without labelling, and each time coming to this feeling of 'Knowing'. By asking the question 'who is knowing this', attention naturally comes back to the state of Knowing, to the Source.

असङ्गस्सच्चिदानन्दः स्वप्रभो द्वैतवर्जितः ।
अस्मीति शब्दविद्धोऽयं समाधिस्सविकल्पकः ॥

asaṅgas-saccidānandaḥ svaprabho dvaita-varjitaḥ
asmīti śabda-viddho-'yaṃ samādhis-savikalpakaḥ

I am free from attachment,
absolute Truth-Consciousness-Bliss,
self-illuminating and beyond duality.
This is Savikalpa Samadhi, meditation related to words.

asaṅgaḥ – without attachment, alone, free
saccidānandaḥ – Truth – Consciousness – Bliss
svaprabhaḥ – by its own light, self illuminating
dvaita varjitaḥ – beyond duality • *asmīti* – I am that
śabda viddhaḥ – related to words • *ayaṃ* – this is
samādhiḥ-savikalpakaḥ – the practice of meditation with an object

VERSE 25

In the previous verse, one is asked to experience oneself as Awareness, in which thoughts feelings, emotions etc are appearing and disappearing. In this verse, a contemplation of that Awareness itself is being presented as a practice. One can also call it a practice of affirmation.

Throughout the day words that we use usually take the attention outwards. Even when we think that we are taking the attention inwards, we are still only looking at states of mind. It is a rare event when attention is able to touch the very Source of attention in us.

When somebody pays us a compliment, or is talking about us, we tend to be naturally focussed and attentive. In this verse, compliments are being paid to who one really is. The words here are being used to address the Subject. The energy of the words is turned inwards to shine a light on the light of Consciousness. To those people, in whom some awakening has happened, these words are not just words, rather drops of nectar falling in the ears.

The word '*Asanga*' means without relationship, alone, detached. The characters in a movie are related to each other according to the script. The characters are not free, and are dependant on the actions of the other characters. The screen on which the movie is playing, on the other hand, exists before, during and after the movie.

In the same way events appearing in Consciousness exist in relation to previous events, but Consciousness itself, exists beyond the events. '*Asanga*' does not mean that one does not have relationships, and one is not involved with life, rather it means that one also exists in another dimension, which is empty and pristine.

This ability to engage with life, and yet experience a dimension free of limitations, is the art of living.

The other meaning of '*Asanga*' is to be free of one's own thoughts. The relationships are not just external. In fact the really dangerous relationship, is the identification with one's own fears, hopes, desires and anxieties.

Satchitananda has been described in previous verses as Being-

Consciousness-Bliss. 'Being' is 'Existence' which is beyond birth and death. 'Consciousness' means the 'Light' in which the world is seen. '*Ananda*' means that 'Bliss' which is beyond happiness and unhappiness.

'*Sva*' means self and '*prabha*' means light. '*Svaprabho*' means that one is one's own light. The Light of Lights. To see the sunlight, first you have to be there, you have to be conscious. A beautiful moon can only be seen when there is the light of Consciousness to experience it.

This light of Consciousness, in which the world is appearing, is the greatest miracle.

'*Dvaita-varjitah*' means free of duality. That, which is aware of duality, is itself not duality. Duality is the basis of all hostility, just as Oneness is the basis of Love. When there is duality in a relationship, there is a feeling of 'otherness', a feeling of alienation.

In different relationships, one tries to find a feeling of Oneness. People get married, join groups, join gangs, join clubs, join the army, go to parties etc to find this experience.

'*Dvaita-varjitah*' is pointing to who one is at the Source. In this Source, the entire universe is seen as appearing in oneself. It is actually a state of incredible intimacy, in which there is nobody other than Self. There is no duality left to be free of.

स्वानुभूतिरसावेशाद् दृश्यशब्दावुपेक्ष्य तु ।
निर्विकल्पस्समाधिस्स्यात् निवातस्थित–दीपवत् ॥

svānubhūti-rasāveśād dṛśya-śabdāvupekṣya tu
nirvikalpas-samādhissyāt nivāta-sthita-dīpavat

Absorbed in the experience of one's Self,
drawn inwards by the Bliss in the heart,
having transcended the world of forms and sounds,
is the experience of Nirvikalpa Samadhi.
Here awareness is steady like the flame of a lamp in a windless place.

svānubhūti – Self experiencing Self • *rasāveśād* – absorbed in Bliss
dṛśya-śabdāu – both forms and sounds
upekṣya – indifferent, transcending • *tu* – but
nirvikalpas-samādhiḥ – meditation without any object • *syāt* – is
nivāta-sthita – not disturbed by air • *dīpavat* – like an oil lamp

VERSE 26

'*Sva*' means Self and '*Anubhuti*' means experience. '*Sva-anubhuti*' means the Self experiencing Self.

In all the experiences of one's life, there is a subject/object relationship. When Self is experiencing Self, there is only one Self. All the words used to describe this non-dual experience, are made up of duality, and therefore useless. It happens when it happens.

Only Self remains, only Awareness remains.

In the previous verse, Self is described as *Ananda* or Bliss. In this verse, Self is described as '*Rasa*'. *Ananda* and *Rasa* are synonyms for the same experience. *Rasa* means juice, an intense pleasure. *Rasa* is another word for Self-experience. In fact, it is said that other than Self there is no *Rasa*. Whenever one is happy or feels drawn to happiness, one is actually being drawn to the *Rasa* within.

In Indian philosophy, it is not the object one craves that

gives satisfaction once attained, but the *Rasa*, associated with that object. The addictions are not to alcohol, drugs, sex or shopping, but to the experience of the *Rasa* associated with them. When the *Rasa* is gone, we tend to lose interest in that person or that object.

A stray dog chewing on a bone imagines the bone to be juicy. In reality, the edges of the bone are piercing its gums, and the resulting blood is what it is finding so tasty. So it is with all second hand experiences of happiness. One imagines objects and people to be source of *Rasa*, when in fact, it is our own Juice that we are experiencing.

Rasa is the Self, *Rasa* is Awareness. Going directly to the Source of *Rasa* is first hand happiness. Self is experiencing its own True Nature as *Rasa*. *Rasa* is the juice of Ecstasy.

In this verse, *Shankaracharya* is speaking to an advanced practitioner. The mind of such a person is pulled strongly to the Source within. People have described this as a powerful force that one could not possibly resist. Such a person leaves behind meditation practices, associated with the seen, and with sounds.

To have found the Source of this ecstatic Juice makes one oblivious to the pleasures offered by the world. It is not that one does not want pleasure, rather one has found a direct pipeline to the vast ocean of pleasure.

In this verse the Consciousness of such a being, is compared to the flame of an oil lamp, in a place free from any wind. The mind becomes completely steady. In Indian philosophy this is the only way to bring the mind to a state of peace. The mind runs here and there only in search of pleasure. All the unsteadiness is due to the search for happiness.

When Consciousness returns to the Source, the purpose of the search finally comes to an end. One sinks ever deeper into one's Truth.

हृदीव बाह्यदेशेऽपि यस्मिन् कस्मिंश्च वस्तुनि ।
समाधिराद्यस्सन्मात्रात् नामरूपपृथक्कृतिः ॥

hṛdīva bāhyadeśe-'pi yasmin kasmiṃśca vastuni
samādhir-ādyas-sanmātrāt nāmarūpa-pṛthakkṛtiḥ

The first Samadhih can be practiced using any object,
anywhere, in the heart or outside, by simply separating
the underlying Truth from the name and form.

hrdīva – in the heart • *bāhya* – outside • *deśe* – place • *api* – also
yasmin kasmiṃśca vastuni – in any thing
samādhiḥ – meditation in possible • *ādyah* – the first
sat mātrāt – from the underlying Truth • *nāma rūpa* – name and form
pṛthakkṛtiḥ – the act of separating

VERSE 27

The first words '*Hridiva bahyadese'pi*' mean 'in the internal space or the external space'. In other words, this practice can be done with internal objects or external objects, with the eyes closed or the eyes open. In the heart or outside.

The expression '*Yasmin kasminsca vastuni*' means 'this thing, that thing or anything'. One can focus on any object, mental or physical, internal or external, big or small, sacred or profane. The practice now is to separate the name and form of that object, from the underlying Existence, from *Sat*. This practice is not an intellectual practice of affirmation; it is a practice of looking at an object with great intensity, and cutting through the form.

During the *Yoga* practice, one can take one's attention to any place in the body during the *Asana*, to activate Consciousness. If one focuses on tension, it will dissolve. If one focuses on the breath, just the attention, will transform the breath. If one brings the attention to a stiffness or an injury, healing will happen. The *Nama Rupa* dissolves and Consciousness remains.

Looking at something with attention, one may find the concreteness of that object melting. Solid objects may appear not so solid. One may experience colours in a different way. These are all signs of penetrating the 'hard shell' of name and form. Name and form is like a rigid outer layer and seems so real, that in the early days, even to challenge the delusion may seem insane.

One may start to look right through a person, as if that person were transparent. It may seem as if the body were just made up of particles of light, and as if the body of the one who is looking, is also made up only of light. All apparent solidity of form, time and location may take on a different quality.

This is a wonderful verse for people who are practicing *Yoga* regularly. When one comes out of a *Yoga* session, one feels a lot of space has opened. Instead of filling up the space immediately with stuff, one can use this energy to look deeply for a few minutes at any object. It could be a bicycle, a tree by the road, a person or anything.

Looking deeply, means simply looking without distraction, and also looking without tension. Looking without trying to understand. Looking at the ‘Isness’ of a thing. Looking at its Existence aspect. Looking at the form without coming to a conclusion.

In this practice one is not being asked to believe something but simply to learn to look, and then to see what happens.

अखण्डैकरसं वस्तु सच्चिदानन्द-लक्षणम्।
इत्यविच्छिन्न-चिन्तेयं समाधिर्मध्यमो भवेत्॥

akhaṇḍaika-rasaṃ vastu saccidānanda lakṣaṇam
ityavicchinna-cinteyaṃ samādhir-madhyamo bhavet

Reality is unbroken, undivided, is composed of one Essence,
and is of the nature of Satchitananda.
This uninterrupted contemplation is Samadhi of the middle kind.

akhaṇḍaḥ – unbroken, undivided
eka-rasaṃ – one Juice, one Essence • *vastu* – Reality
satcitānanda – Truth – Existence – Bliss • *lakṣaṇam* – pointing to
avicchinna – uninterrupted • *cinta* – contemplation
samādhiḥ – meditation • *madhyamaḥ* – middle kind • *bhavet* – is

VERSE 28

This verse talks about a middle kind of *Samadhi*.This could mean something between *Savikalpa* and *Nirvikalpa*, or a combination of both. It could be an affirmation or it could mean an actual experience.

This verse says that everything that exists, is only made of one Essence.The nature of everything is *Satchitananda*. One Juice is flowing directly from the Source.

Sat means that Truth, which is beyond truth and untruth. *Sat* also means that Life, which is beyond life and death. *Chit* means the Knowing Principle, Awareness and Self Awareness. It also means Awareness of one's Existence. *Ananda* means Bliss, Ecstasy, Love, *Rasa*. It means that Love, which is beyond love and hate, it means the Beauty, which is beyond beauty and ugliness, the Joy which is beyond joy and sorrow.

In other words, the unconditional Love that all are seeking, is one's own Essence.

In this verse one is asked to walk through life with a conviction, an uncompromising recognition of the Oneness behind all experiences.

Instead of calling a tree, a tree, one says '*Satchitananda* manifesting as a tree'. Hearing the sound of a bird, this same feeling that '*Satchitananda* is manifesting as the birdsong'. Seeing a stone by the side of the road and feeling that '*Satchitananda* is manifesting as the stone'.

Seeing everything as One, from the most mundane, to the most exalted, becomes the practice. People who are religious by nature may experience this as a feeling that God is everywhere, everything is touched by God, there is no place that God is not.

स्तब्धीभावो रसास्वादात् तृतीयः पूर्ववन्मतः ।
एतैः समाधिभिः षड्भिः नयेत् कालं निरन्तरम् ॥

stabdhī-bhāvo rasāsvādāt tṛtīyaḥ pūrvavan-mataḥ
etaiḥ samādhibhiḥ ṣaḍbhiḥ nayet kālaṃ nirantaram

Total stillness, when one is absorbed in the taste of Bliss,
is the third kind of Samadhi as described before.
Time should be used to always practice these six Samadhis.

stabdh bhāvah – total stillness
rasā svādāt – the taste of inner Bliss • *tṛtīyaḥ* – third kind
pūrvavat – as previously • *mataḥ* – described • *etaiḥ* – with these
samādhibhiḥ – meditations • *ṣaḍbhiḥ* – six • *nayet* – should spend
kālaṃ – time • *nirantaram* – always, continuously

VERSE 29

If one takes the juice out of a mango, there is nothing left of the mango. If one takes the juice away from any experience, the experience becomes dull or dead.

Using the word 'Juice' for Self is a way of saying that whatever beauty, joy or happiness, that is experienced in any event, is really one's own Self. That, which one is seeking outside in experiences, is present as one's own Self.

What the *Yogi* is seeking, and what a so-called worldly person is seeking, is exactly the same. Both are seeking *Rasa*. The person in the world projects the *Rasa* outwards onto external objects, and then pursues them. The *Yogi* seeks the same *Rasa* at its Source, in himself. In the inner search one discovers *Rasa* in its Unconditioned State.

This ending of the search for *Rasa*, by finding the Source, is called Liberation.

Renunciation means, not to renounce the *Rasa*, but to stop

seeking it outside. Renunciation means the renunciation of externalization.

The *Nirvikalpa Samadhi* spoken of in verse 26 is re-iterated here. '*Stabdhi Bhava*' is the experience of total Stillness. '*Rasa Svadat*' means the taste of the Juice. As the attention moves deeper towards the very Source of attention, intense experiences of Bliss start to arise.

There is an expression '*Soundarya Lahari*', which means waves of beauty, waves of joy. As these waves of Bliss arise in oneself, the attention does not want to go anywhere else, even for a moment. The slightest movement starts to feel like a disturbance.

These waves of Bliss may start as a very gentle inner caress. So subtle, one may miss them at first, and just have a general sense of wellbeing. As the attention and stillness develop, these waves may be felt as encompassing everything internal and external. One may feel as if there is nothing but waves of Bliss, waves of Light. These waves are made up of Stillness and merge back into Stillness.

In the next line, *Shankaracharya* says that one can practise any one, or all six of these practices. In a sense these practices are just methods of shifting the way of looking. There is really no practice here. No *Asanas*, no *Pranayama*, no chanting. Just learning to look in a different way. A different perspective.

These six *Samadhis* are meant for different people of different natures, and at different stages in their practice. Continuity in the practice is most important and one should use one's time to experiment with them.

देहाभिमाने गलिते विज्ञाते परमात्मनि ।
यत्र-यत्र मनो याति तत्र-तत्र समाधयः ॥

dehābhimāne galite vijñāte paramātmani
yatra yatra mano yāti tatra tatra samādhayaḥ

When body identification has dissolved,
the Supreme Self is realized.
In that state, wherever the mind goes
there is only the experience of Samadhi.

dehābhimāne – identification with the body •
galite – melts, dissolves • *vijñāte* – is known •
paramātmani – the Supreme Self •
yatra yatra – wherever, wherever • *manaḥ* – the mind •
yāti – goes • *tatra tatra* – there, there •
samādhayaḥ – is Samadhi

VERSE 30

In these last two verses the flowering of the practice is described.

'*Deha-abhimane*' means identification with the body. It means thinking oneself to be a body that is born and dies. It means believing oneself to be the bundle of thoughts that are moving in the head. In this verse, it is said that the practice reduces this habit of constantly identifying with the physical and mental activities.

The word '*Galite*' means to be cooked, to become soft, to melt. When the feeling of being a hard, substantial, solidified ego melts, the highest Vision appears spontaneously.

'*Vijnate Paramatmani*' means to know the highest Reality.

The first line of this verse says that the melting of the ego-self is the same as the realization of Truth. These are not two separate events. The dilemma in all spiritual practices is that the conditioned self sets out in search of the Unconditioned, but can never reach its goal. The conditioned can never know the Unconditioned. The conditioned can only melt, get out of the way, and the realization of the Unconditioned happens naturally. They are one event.

The second line is a masterpiece. It says that in this state, wherever the mind goes, wherever the attention goes, wherever the body goes, the experience of *Samadhi* is ever-present. It is like saying that no matter how far an aeroplane flies it cannot fly out of space.

Once the Totality has been revealed, the concepts of coming and going, no longer apply. One cannot go anywhere, where the Totality is not.

Even the highest *Nirvikalpa Samadhi* is said to have a beginning and an end. This verse is an example of *Sahaja Samadhi*, in which there is no beginning and no end.

One just becomes quiet. This is *Chup Sadhana*. The underlying Reality is revealed. All is arising in Awareness, as Awareness.

भिद्यते हृदय-ग्रन्थिः छिद्यन्ते सर्वसंशयाः ।
क्षीयन्ते चास्य कर्माणि तस्मिन् दृष्टे परावरे ॥

bhidyate hṛdaya-granthiḥ chidyante sarva-saṃśayāḥ
kṣīyante cāsya karmāṇi tasmin dṛṣṭe parāvare

The knot of the heart is cut, all doubts disappear,
and the effects of karma get exhausted,
in this vision of seeing the Totality.

bhidyate – is cut • *hṛdaya-granthiḥ* – the Knot of the Heart
chidyante – are resolved, eliminated
sarva-saṃśayāḥ – all the doubts • *kṣīyante* – get exhausted
āsya – of this • *karmāṇi* – all the karmas • *tasmin* – that
dṛṣṭe – having seen • *parāvare* – who is everywhere

VERSE 31

'*Hridaya Granthi*' refers to the knot in the heart. It is said that the point where the Formless and the form connect is like a knot. This is the knot of the Seer and the seen.

This knot is also called the '*Jada-chetan Granthi*', which means the place where Consciousness is tied with the material. This knot is the *Ahamkara*, as the conditioned self.

When this knot in the heart is loosened *Ahamkara*, the personal identity, melts into Consciousness. Only impersonal Consciousness now remains. The limitations of being a separate self fall away. Self is experienced as Unbounded Awareness.

'*Chidyante sarva samshayah*' means all the doubts are cut. In practice, the disappearance of the doubter, who is the conditioned self, is the cutting of all the doubts. The doubts cannot remain without a doubter.

The head has surrendered. The heart is free.

'*Ksiyante casya karmani*' means all actions and reactions come to an end. It does not mean that one stops eating, drinking, walking, talking or fulfilling the obligations of day-to-day life. It just means that the result of actions from previous lifetimes and the compulsive actions of this lifetime, come to an end. The conditioned self, this feeling of a 'me' that has to do this and has to do that, is no longer there.

Thoughts of actions arise in the heart and translate themselves into what needs to be done. People have said that it feels like 'God's Will' is operating in all actions. These actions now do not leave behind any residue. No new Karma is created.

The *Hridakash* or 'Sky of the Heart' is revealed. This *Hridakash* is forever Free, Unbounded and Infinite.

The marriage of Seer and seen happens.

This is a State of Grace.

All that is, is Awareness.

DṚG DṚYŚA VIVEKA

VERSES FOR CHANTING

1

rūpaṃ dṛśyaṃ locanaṃ dṛk tad dṛśyaṃ dṛk tu mānasam
dṛśyā dhīvṛttayas-sākṣī dṛgeva na tu dṛśyate

2

nīla-pīta-sthūla-sūkṣma-hṛa sva-dīrghādi bhedataḥ
nānāvidhāni rūpāṇi paśyel-locanam-ekadhā

3

āndhya-māndya-paṭutveṣu netradharmeṣu caikadhā
saṃkalpayen-manaḥ srotra-tvagādau yojyatām idam

4

kāmaḥ saṃkalpa-saṃdehau śraddhā-'śraddhe dhṛtītare
hrīr-dhīr-bhīr-ityevam-ādīn bhāsayaty ekadhā citiḥ

5

nodeti nāstmetyeṣā na vṛddhiṃ yāti na kṣayam
svayaṃ vibhātyathānyāni bhāsayet sādhanaṃ vinā

6

cicchāyā'-veśato-buddhau bhānaṃ dhī stu dvidhā sthitā
ekāhaṁ-kṛtiranyā syāt antaḥkaraṇa-rūpiṇī

7

chāyā'haṁkārayor-aikyaṃ taptāyaḥ piṇḍavan-matam
tadahaṁkāra-tādātmyāt dehaś-cetanatām-agāt

8

ahaṁkārasya tādātmyaṃ cicchāyā deha sākṣibhiḥ
sahajaṃ karmajaṃ bhrāntijanyaṃ ca trividhaṃ kramāt

9

saṃbandhinos-sator-nāsti nivṛttis-sahajasya tu
karma-kṣayāt prabodhāt ca nivartete kramād-ubhe

10

ahaṁkāra laye suptau bhavet deho-'pyacetanaḥ
ahaṁkāra vikāsārdhaḥ svapnas-sarvastu jāgaraḥ

11

antaḥkaraṇa-vṛttiśca citicchāyaikyam-āgatā
vāsanāḥ kalpayet svapne bodhe-'kṣairviṣayān bahiḥ

12

mano-'haṃkṛtyupādānaṃ liṅgamekaṃ jaḍātmakam
avasthātrayam-anveti jāyate mriyate tathā

13

śakti-dvayaṃ hi māyāyā vikṣepāvṛti rūpakam
vikṣepaśaktir-lingādi brahmāṇḍ-antaṃ jagat sṛjet

14

sṛṣṭir nāma brahmarūpe saccidānanda-vastuni
abdhau phenādivat sarva-nāma-rūpa-prasāraṇā

15

antar-dṛkdṛśyayor-bhedaṃ bahiśca brahma sargayoḥ
āvṛṇotyaparā śaktiḥ sā saṃsārasya kāraṇam

16

sākṣiṇah purato bhāti liṅgaṃ dehena saṃyutam
citicchāyā samāveśāt jīvaḥ syād vyāvahārikaḥ

17

asya jīvatvam-āropāt sākṣiṇyapyavabhāsate
āvṛtau tu vinaṣṭāyāṃ bhede bhāte-'payāti tat

18

tathā sarga-brahmaṇośca bhedam-āvṛtya tiṣṭhati
yā śaktis-tadvaśād-brahma vikṛtatvena bhāsate

19

atrāpyāvṛti-nāśena vibhāti brahma-sargayoḥ
bhedastayor-vikāraḥ syāt sarge na brahmaṇi kvacit

20

asti bhāti priyaṃ rūpaṃ nāma cetyaṃśa-pañcakam
ādyatrayaṃ brahma rūpaṃ jagad rūpaṃ tato dvayam

21

khavāyvagni-jalorvīṣu devatiryaṅ-narādiṣu
abhinnās-saccidānandāḥ bhidyate rupanāmanī

22

upekṣya nāmarūpe dve saccidānanda-tatparaḥ
samādhiṃ sarvadā kuryād hṛdaye vā-'thavā bahiḥ

23

savikalpo nirvikalpaḥ samādhir-dvividho hṛdi
dṛśya śabdānuviddhena savikalpaḥ punar-dvidhā

24

kāmādyāś-cittagā dṛśyāḥ tatsākṣitvena cetanam
dhyāyet dṛśyānu-viddho-'yaṃ samādhiḥ savikalpakaḥ

25

asaṅgas-saccidānandaḥ svaprabho dvaita-varjitaḥ
asmīti śabda-viddho-'yaṃ samādhis-savikalpakaḥ

26

svānubhūti-rasāveśād dṛśya-śabdāvupekṣya tu
nirvikalpas-samādhissyāt nivāta-sthita-dīpavat

27

hṛdīva bāhyadeśe-'pi yasmin kasmiṃśca vastuni
samādhir-ādyas-sanmātrāt nāmarūpa-pṛthakkṛtiḥ

28

akhaṇḍaika-rasaṃ vastu saccidānanda lakṣaṇam
ityavicchinna-cinteyaṃ samādhir-madhyamo bhavet

29

stabdhī-bhāvo rasāsvādāt tṛtīyaḥ pūrvavan-mataḥ
etaiḥ samādhibhiḥ ṣaḍbhiḥ nayet kālaṃ nirantaram

30

dehābhimāne galite vijñāte paramātmani
yatra yatra mano yāti tatra tatra samādhayaḥ

31

bhidyate hṛdaya-granthiḥ chidyante sarva-saṃśayāḥ
kṣīyante cāsya karmāṇi tasmin dṛṣṭe parāvare

ABOUT THE AUTHOR

Clarissa was born in Austria in 1956, and from early childhood lived in different countries around the world. After completing her postgraduate studies at the Royal College of Art in 1981, Clarissa spent several years travelling in Thailand, Burma and Indonesia, and lived in India for many years. This was a time of exploration in the world of art and design.

Throughout her life, Clarissa has explored many different spiritual traditions, and has worked with various teachers. In the early years, the focus was on *Sufi*, *Buddhist* and *Dzogchen* teachings. Later on *Yoga* and *Vipassana* meditation have become the main practice.

Her inner journey really took off when she started practicing *Yoga*, and met her teacher Mansoor, with whom she has been working closely for the last ten years. A vast new horizon opened up for her with the study of scripture, and she was able to recognize the experiences she was having in her own *Yoga* practice, in this wider context.

Clarissa has been teaching *Yoga* since 2002 in India and Europe. She is currently based between Brighton and India.

For any further information or feedback on this book please contact:

yoga@chup-sadhana.com
www.chup-sadhana.com

10960950R00102

Printed in Great Britain
by Amazon.co.uk, Ltd.,
Marston Gate.